Keeping Score for All

The Effects of Inclusion and Accommodation Policies on Large-Scale Educational Assessments

Committee on Participation of English Language Learners and
Students with Disabilities in NAEP and Other Large-Scale Assessments

Judith Anderson Koenig and Lyle F. Bachman, Editors

Board on Testing and Assessment
Center for Education
Division of Behavioral and Social Sciences and Education

NATIONAL RESEARCH COUNCIL
OF THE NATIONAL ACADEMIES

THE NATIONAL ACADEMIES PRESS
Washington, D.C.
www.nap.edu

THE NATIONAL ACADEMIES PRESS 500 Fifth Street, N.W. Washington, DC 20001

NOTICE: The project that is the subject of this report was approved by the Governing Board of the National Research Council, whose members are drawn from the councils of the National Academy of Sciences, the National Academy of Engineering, and the Institute of Medicine. The members of the committee responsible for the report were chosen for their special competences and with regard for appropriate balance.

This study was supported by Contract/Grant No. R215U990016 between the National Academy of Sciences and the U.S. Department of Education. Any opinions, findings, conclusions, or recommendations expressed in this publication are those of the author(s) and do not necessarily reflect the views of the organizations or agencies that provided support for the project.

Library of Congress Cataloging-in-Publication Data

National Research Council (U.S.). Committee on Participation of English Language Learners and Students with Disabilities in NAEP and Other Large-Scale Assessments.

Keeping score for all : the effects of inclusion and accommodation policies on large-scale educational assessments / Committee on Participation of English Language Learners and Students with Disabilities in NAEP and Other Large-Scale Assessments ; Judith Anderson Koenig and Lyle F. Bachman, editors.

p. cm.

Includes bibliographical references.

ISBN 0-309-09253-1 (pbk.) — ISBN 0-309-53317-1 (pdf)

1. Educational tests and measurements—United States—Evaluation. 2. Inclusive education—United States—Evaluation. 3. Students with disabilities—Education—United States. 4. Limited English-proficient students—Education—United States. 5. National Assessment of Educational Progress (Project) I. Koenig, Judith A. II. Bachman, Lyle F., 1944- III. Title.

LB3060.83.N295 2004

371.26'4—dc22

2004014364

Additional copies of this report are available from the National Academies Press, 500 Fifth Street, N.W., Lockbox 285, Washington, DC 20055; (800) 624-6242 or (202) 334-3313 (in the Washington metropolitan area); Internet, http://www.nap.edu.

Printed in the United States of America

Suggested citation: National Research Council. (2004). *Keeping Score for All: The Effects of Inclusion and Accommodation Policies on Large-Scale Educational Assessments.* Committee on Participation of English Language Learners and Students with Disabilities in NAEP and Other Large-Scale Assessments. Judith A. Koenig and Lyle F. Bachman, Editors. Board on Testing and Assessment, Center for Education, Division of Behavioral and Social Sciences and Education. Washington, DC: The National Academies Press.

THE NATIONAL ACADEMIES
Advisers to the Nation on Science, Engineering, and Medicine

The **National Academy of Sciences** is a private, nonprofit, self-perpetuating society of distinguished scholars engaged in scientific and engineering research, dedicated to the furtherance of science and technology and to their use for the general welfare. Upon the authority of the charter granted to it by the Congress in 1863, the Academy has a mandate that requires it to advise the federal government on scientific and technical matters. Dr. Bruce M. Alberts is president of the National Academy of Sciences.

The **National Academy of Engineering** was established in 1964, under the charter of the National Academy of Sciences, as a parallel organization of outstanding engineers. It is autonomous in its administration and in the selection of its members, sharing with the National Academy of Sciences the responsibility for advising the federal government. The National Academy of Engineering also sponsors engineering programs aimed at meeting national needs, encourages education and research, and recognizes the superior achievements of engineers. Dr. Wm. A. Wulf is president of the National Academy of Engineering.

The **Institute of Medicine** was established in 1970 by the National Academy of Sciences to secure the services of eminent members of appropriate professions in the examination of policy matters pertaining to the health of the public. The Institute acts under the responsibility given to the National Academy of Sciences by its congressional charter to be an adviser to the federal government and, upon its own initiative, to identify issues of medical care, research, and education. Dr. Harvey V. Fineberg is president of the Institute of Medicine.

The **National Research Council** was organized by the National Academy of Sciences in 1916 to associate the broad community of science and technology with the Academy's purposes of furthering knowledge and advising the federal government. Functioning in accordance with general policies determined by the Academy, the Council has become the principal operating agency of both the National Academy of Sciences and the National Academy of Engineering in providing services to the government, the public, and the scientific and engineering communities. The Council is administered jointly by both Academies and the Institute of Medicine. Dr. Bruce M. Alberts and Dr. Wm. A. Wulf are chair and vice chair, respectively, of the National Research Council.

www.national-academies.org

COMMITTEE ON PARTICIPATION OF ENGLISH LANGUAGE LEARNERS AND STUDENTS WITH DISABILITIES IN NAEP AND OTHER LARGE-SCALE ASSESSMENTS

Lyle F. Bachman *(Chair*)*, Department of Applied Linguistics, University of California, Los Angeles
Jonathan G. Dings, Boulder Valley School District, Boulder, CO
Judy L. Elliott, Long Beach Unified School District, San Pedro, CA
Margaret J. McLaughlin, Institute for the Study of Exceptional Children and Youth, University of Maryland, College Park
Mark D. Reckase *(Chair**)*, Measurement and Quantitative Methods, Michigan State University
Lourdes C. Rovira, Miami-Dade County Public Schools, Miami, FL
María Medina Seidner, Texas Education Agency, Austin, TX
Rebecca Zwick, Gevirtz Graduate School of Education, University of California, Santa Barbara

Judith A. Koenig, *Study Director*
Alexandra Beatty, *Senior Program Officer*
Michael DeCarmine, *Senior Program Assistant*

---

*Beginning November 2003.
**Stepped down from the Committee in November 2003, when he was appointed to the National Assessment Governing Board.

Preface

The Committee on the Participation of Students with Disabilities and English Language Learners in NAEP and Other Large-Scale Assessments was formed under the auspices of the National Research Council (NRC) with the support of the National Center for Education Statistics (NCES). Its report addresses critical issues in the assessment of students with disabilities and English language learners, an issue that has come to the forefront of conversations about the effects of the No Child Left Behind Act of 2001. The NRC's Board on Testing and Assessment (BOTA) has focused considerable attention during its ten-year history on the challenges and questions presented by the need to include these students in assessment and accountability programs. At present these students make up approximately 20 percent of the nation's 46 million public school students, and while the responsibility for monitoring their progress is not new either to the National Assessment of Educational Progress (NAEP) or to states and districts, the provisions of the No Child Left Behind Act of 2001 have made that responsibility more public, more complex, and more urgent.

A November 2001 BOTA workshop, also sponsored by NCES, focused on the reporting and interpretation of test results for students with disabilities and English language learners who receive test accommodations. Discussions at the workshop made clear that several key issues merited more in-depth examination. The first set of concerns pertained to the way decisions regarding both the inclusion of students with special needs in assessments and the identification of appropriate accommodations for them are made. It was clear from the workshop not only that there is considerable variability across states and districts in the way these decisions are made but also that this variability can affect NAEP results in significant ways. The second set of concerns pertained to the research that has been conducted on the effects of accommodations on test performance. The 2001 workshop stimulated considerable discussion about the conclusions that could be drawn from the existing literature base and about appropriate research approaches for evaluating the effects of accommodations on test performance.

Therefore, at the request of NCES, the Committee on the Participation of Students with Disabilities and English Language Learners in NAEP and Other Large-Scale Assessments was formed and given a three-part charge, to (1) synthesize research findings about the effects of accommodations on test performance, (2) review the procedures used for making inclusion and accommodation decisions for large-scale assessment programs, and (3) determine the implications of these findings for NAEP inclusions and accommodation policies. The work of this committee was intended to build on the discussions from the 2001 workshop (and other earlier NRC projects).

Thus, the report from the 2001 workshop served as the starting point for the committee's work. In addition, researcher Stephen Sireci was commissioned to conduct a review and critique of the research literature on the effects of accommodations on test performance. This literature review focused on empirical studies conducted between 1990 and 2003 and was commissioned and completed in time to be ready for the committee's first meeting in March 2003. The workshop report and this literature review served as background information for the committee as it began its in-depth examination of the relevant policies and practices in effect around the country and the state of the research in this vital area.

The resulting report is designed to set the committee's findings and recommendations in the context of current policy and practice with regard to the inclusion and accommodation of students with disabilities and English language learners. In this report, the committee discusses the meaning of scores from accommodated assessments and the kinds of evidence that are needed to support inferences made from these scores. It is BOTA's hope that this report will be of use to both the officials who oversee NAEP and those who oversee state and local assessments as they work to make their assessments as inclusive as possible, and to make them yield results that accurately reflect the knowledge and skills of all students.

The committee is very grateful to the many individuals who have helped with this project from its inception. It takes particular note of the contribution of Mark Reckase of Michigan State University, who served as its chair through most of its work, until his appointment to the National Assessment Governing Board required him to step down. The committee also sincerely appreciates Lyle Bachman's willingness to assume the responsibility of chair for the completion of the project.

The committee extends its heartfelt thanks to Peggy Carr of NCES for her interest in this important topic and her willingness to fund the project. The committee also thanks Arnold Goldstein of NCES for his constant and prompt support and quick answers to all of the committee's questions. The committee also appreciates the assistance of Debra Hollinger Martinez, formerly of NCES, who provided valuable materials and information. Nancy Caldwell of Westat provided information about NAEP's sampling procedures and responded to committee questions about NAEP's administrative procedures for accommodating students with disabilities and English language learners. Jim Carlson of NAGB provided the committee with information on NAEP policies on accommodation as well as on research on the effects of accommodations on NAEP results. Mary Crovo of NAGB spoke with the committee about the constructs assessed by NAEP, and the committee is grateful to all of these busy officials for their time and assistance.

Many others assisted the committee as well. Researchers Martha Thurlow of the National Center on Education Outcomes and Charlene Rivera of the Center for Equity and Excellence provided the committee with background about states' policies; John Olsen of the Council of Chief State School Officers (CCSSO) made a presentation about the results of the CCSSO's annual survey of states' practices. Presentations by Wayne Camara of the College Board and Robert Ziomek of ACT, Inc., on their research on the effects of accommodations on admissions test performance were particularly informative. The committee is grateful to Ed Haertel of Stanford University for providing an advance copy of his paper on evidentiary arguments and the comparability of scores from standard and nonstandard test administrations. Eric Hansen of Educational Testing Service briefed the committee on his work on the evidence-centered design approach and prepared a commissioned paper that was very helpful to the committee. The committee is also indebted to Stephen Sireci of the University of Massachusetts, Amherst and his colleagues Stanley Scarpati and Shuhong Li for their work on the commissioned review and critique of the literature.

The committee also wishes to thank the NRC staff who have supported the project. Study director Judith Koenig has offered leadership and support in countless ways and has guided the committee through some quite complicated territory. The committee also thanks Pasquale DeVito for his initial work on the project, and Stuart Elliott and Patricia Morison, who read and made valuable comments on several versions of the report. Michael DeCarmine's calm and able administrative assistance throughout the project is much appreciated as well. The committee is also grateful for Alexandra Beatty's expert writing ability. She provided invaluable assistance in drafting portions of the report and editing it so that it read with one voice. NRC editor Chris McShane provided valuable editing and smoothing in the final stages as well. Finally, the committee is indebted to Kirsten Sampson Snyder for ably guiding the report through the NRC review process.

This report has been reviewed in draft form by individuals chosen for their diverse perspectives and technical expertise, in accordance with procedures approved by the NRC's RRC. The purpose of this independent review is to provide candid and critical comments that will assist the institution in making its published report as sound as possible and ensuring that the report meets institutional standards for objectivity, evidence, and responsiveness to the study charge. The review comments and draft manuscript remain confidential to protect the integrity of the deliberative process. I thank the following individuals for their review of this report: Jamal Abedi, Technical Projects, Center for the Study of Evaluation, University of California, Los Angeles; Susan A. Agruso, Office of Assessment, Charlotte-Mecklenburg School District, Charlotte, NC; Richard Duran, Gevirtz Graduate School of Education, University of California, Santa Barbara; Shelley Loving-Ryder, Assistant Superintendent for Assessment and Reporting, Virginia Department of Education; Diana Pullin, Education Law and Public Policy, Boston College; and Martha Thurlow, National Center on Educational Outcomes, University of Minnesota, Minneapolis.

Although the reviewers listed above have provided many constructive comments and suggestions, they were not asked to endorse the conclusions or recommendations, nor did they see the final draft of the report before its release. The review of this report was overseen by Lyle V. Jones, L.L. Thurstone Psychometric Laboratory, University of North Carolina. Appointed by the National Research Council, he was responsible for making certain that an independent examination of this report was carried out in accordance with institutional procedures and that all review comments were carefully considered. Responsibility for the final content of this report rests entirely with the authoring committee and the institution.

Eva L. Baker
Chair, Board on Testing and Assessment

Contents

Keeping Score for All

The Effects of Inclusion and Accommodation
Policies on Large-Scale Educational Assessments

Executive Summary

U.S. public schools are responsible for educating large numbers of students with disabilities and English language learners—some 20 percent of the nation's 46 million public school students fall into one or both of these categories. Both of these populations have been increasing, and the demand for evidence of their academic progress has also grown. In response to both changing public expectations and legal mandates, the federal government, states, and districts have attempted to include more such students in educational assessments.

Testing these two groups of students, however, poses particular challenges. Many of these students have attributes—such as physical, emotional, or learning disabilities or limited fluency in English—that may prevent them from readily demonstrating what they know or can do on a test. In order to allow these students to demonstrate their knowledge and skills, testing accommodations are used. For the purpose of this report, we have defined testing accommodations by drawing from the definition in the *AERA/APA/NCME Standards for Educational and Psychological Testing* (American Educational Research Association et al., 1999). Our adapted definition is as follows: accommodation is used as the general term for any action taken in response to a determination that an individual's disability or level of English language development requires a departure from established testing protocol.[1]

---

[1]The actual definition of accommodation in the standards appears in the chapter that deals with the testing of individuals with disabilities and reads as follows: "accommodation is used as the general term for any action taken in response to a determination that an individual's disability requires a departure from established testing protocol" (American Educational Research Association et al., 1999, p. 101).

The No Child Left Behind Act of 2001 has established the goal for states of including all of their students with disabilities and English language learners in their assessments.[2] At the same time, the sponsors of the National Assessment of Educational Progress (NAEP) hope to increase the participation of these groups of students in NAEP assessments. The use of accommodations provides an important means for increasing inclusion rates for these groups. In identifying appropriate accommodations, policy makers must consider the specific characteristics of the test-takers and the nature of the skills and knowledge (referred to as "constructs") to be tested. Effective accommodations should not materially alter the nature of the task or the required response, and they should yield scores that are valid indicators of the constructs being assessed. Both state assessment programs and the sponsors of NAEP have set policies regarding the accommodations they will allow. NAEP also has policies for identifying students who cannot meaningfully participate, even with accommodations, and excluding them from the assessment.

However, the existing base of research about the effects of accommodations on test performance and the comparability of scores obtained under standard and accommodated conditions is insufficient to provide empirical support for many of the decisions that must be made regarding the testing of these students. Thus it has been difficult for both state and NAEP officials to make these decisions, and the result has been considerable variation in what is allowed, both from state to state and between NAEP and the state assessments.[3] These kinds of variations in policy, combined with an insufficient research base, create significant impediments to the interpretation of assessment results for both students with disabilities and English language learners.

STUDY APPROACH

At the request of the U.S. Department of Education, the National Research Council formed the Committee on the Participation of Students with Disabilities and English Language Learners in NAEP and Other Large-Scale Assessments. The charge to the committee was to (1) synthesize research findings about the effects of accommodations on test performance, (2) review the procedures used for making inclusion and accommodation decisions for large-scale assessment programs, and (3) determine the implications of these findings for NAEP inclusion and accommodation policies.

---

[2]The No Child Left Behind Act requires that "not less than 95 percent" of students in each identified subgroup who are enrolled in the school be required to take the assessments used to meet its provisions (P.L. 107-110, Jan. 8, 2002, 115 STAT 1448-1449).

[3]It is important to note that some of this variation can be accounted for by differences in assessment goals, particularly constructs measured, from program to program.

The committee's report addresses three broad areas related to the committee's charge:

1. The policies and practices for the inclusion and provision of accommodations provided for students with disabilities and English language learners that are followed in the National Assessment of Educational Progress and other large-scale assessments conducted by states.
2. The research that has been conducted to date on the effects of accommodations on test performance and the comparability of results from accommodated and standard administrations.
3. The validity of inferences that are made from the results of accommodated assessments.

POLICIES AND PROCEDURES FOR
INCLUSION AND ACCOMMODATION

States' policies and procedures for including students with disabilities and English language learners in large-scale assessments have evolved in recent years, and these policies remain in flux as officials strive to refine their procedures for inclusion and accommodation to comply with legislative mandates. These policies and procedures vary widely from state to state, in part because of differences among assessments and assessment systems, and state policies are different from those used for NAEP assessments.

While NAEP's policies are in many cases different from those in place for state assessments, NAEP results are nevertheless affected by state guidelines in two ways. First, NAEP sampling is based on information from the states regarding the characteristics of all of their students. Thus, the samples used to ensure that the population assessed in NAEP is representative of the nation's student population as a whole are dependent on state policies for classifying students as having a disability or being an English language learner, both because states' classification policies and practices vary and because samples from different states may differ in ways that are not explicitly recognized. Second, once NAEP officials identify the sample of students to be included in the assessment, they provide the schools in which those students are enrolled with guidance as to how to administer the assessment. NAEP officials rely on school-level coordinators, who organize the administration of NAEP at schools, to make consistent and logical decisions about which of the students selected in the original sample can meaningfully participate in the assessment. NAEP officials also rely on school coordinators to make decisions about how participating students will be accommodated, on the basis of their individual needs, NAEP's policies, and the accommodations available in that school.

This variability in policies and procedures is important for several reasons. First, NAEP results are reported separately for states so that comparisons can be made from state to state. If there are differences across states in the characteristics of the sample and in the conditions under which students participate, then the results may not be comparable. Second, national NAEP results are based on the results for each state, so the accuracy of national results is dependent on the consistency of sampling and administration across states. Finally, the policies that govern whether students are included in or excluded from NAEP assessments differ from the policies for inclusion in state assessments. Comparisons of results from a state assessment with those from state NAEP are likely to be affected by these differences.

The accuracy of all data regarding the academic progress of students with disabilities and English language learners is dependent on the uniformity of both the criteria with which students are selected for participation in testing and the administration procedures that are used, including accommodation procedures. In order for the inferences made from assessments of these students to be justifiable, test administration procedures must be uniform. The committee addresses several aspects of this problem with recommendations regarding both policy and research. We address assessment policies first.

The goal of maximizing the participation rates of students with disabilities and English language learners in all testing is widely shared, and is certainly one that the committee endorses. Moreover, the variation in both inclusion and accommodation policies and procedures is too great and has a number of negative effects. The committee therefore makes the following recommendations:[4]

Recommendation 4-1: NAEP officials should

- review the criteria for inclusion and accommodation of students with disabilities and English language learners in light of federal guidelines;
- clarify, elaborate, and revise their criteria as needed; and
- standardize the implementation of these criteria at the school level.

Recommendation 4-2: NAEP officials should work with state assessment directors to review the policies regarding inclusion and accommodation in NAEP assessments and work toward greater consistency between NAEP and state assessment procedures.

Because NAEP is intended to report on the educational progress of students in the United States, it is important to evaluate the extent to which the results fully represent the student population in each state and in the nation. To evaluate this, the committee reviewed policy materials available from NAEP, NAEP reports,

---

[4]The recommendations are numbered according to the chapter in which they are discussed and the sequence in which they appear in each chapter.

and data available from external data sources (e.g., data reported to Congress under the mandates of the Individuals with Disabilities Education Act, data available from the Office of English Language Acquisition, Language Enhancement, and Academic Achievement for Limited English Proficient Students, and U.S. census data). However, our review revealed a number of issues about which we were concerned. First, our review of NAEP policy materials revealed that there is no clear definition of the target population to which NAEP results are intended to generalize. The policy guidance supplied is not sufficiently specific for making judgments about the extent to which inclusion and exclusion decisions affect the generalizability of the results to the targeted population. Specifically, this guidance does not make clear whether it is intended that all students with disabilities and English language learners should be part of the target population or, if not, which of them are excluded. We therefore recommend that:

> **Recommendation 4-3:** NAEP officials should more clearly define the characteristics of the population of students to whom results are intended to generalize. This definition should serve as a guide for decision making and the formulation of regulations regarding inclusion, exclusion, and reporting.

Our review of NAEP reports also revealed that both national and state NAEP reports now indicate the percentages of the NAEP sample that are students with disabilities and English language learners. This is a recent revision to the reports and represents a first step toward making it possible to evaluate the degree to which NAEP samples conform to the definition of the NAEP population. However, the data currently available from state and federal agencies are insufficient to complete the desired comparisons. In the committee's view, it is important to know the extent to which the percentages in the NAEP reports correspond to the percentages of students with disabilities and English language learners reported in other sources. Furthermore, the committee believes that states are undertaking additional efforts at collecting such data, partly in response to the requirements of legislation such as the No Child Left Behind Act of 2001. We encourage all parties (NAEP as well as state and federal agencies) to collect and compile such data so that the desired comparisons can be made. We make two recommendations related to this point:

> **Recommendation 4-4:** NAEP officials should evaluate the extent to which their estimates of the percentages of students with disabilities and English language learners in a state are comparable to similar data collected and reported by states, to the extent feasible given the data that are available. Differences should be investigated to determine the causes.

> **Recommendation 4-5:** Efforts should be made to improve the availability of data about students with disabilities and English language learners. State-

level data are needed that report the total number of English language learners and students with disabilities by grade level in the state. This information should be compiled in a way that allows comparisons to be made across states and should be made readily accessible.

RESEARCH REGARDING ACCOMMODATED ASSESSMENTS

The effects of accommodations on test performance have been researched, but the findings that emerge from the existing research are inconclusive. These findings provide little guidance to those who must make decisions about which accommodations are suitable for particular kinds of students participating in particular assessments. What is lacking is research that directly examines the effects of accommodations on the validity of inferences to be made from scores. Overall, existing research does not provide definitive evidence about which procedures would produce the most valid estimates of performance. Moreover, it does not establish that scores for students with disabilities and English language learners obtained under accommodated conditions are as valid as scores for other students obtained under unaccommodated conditions.

For the most part, existing research focuses on comparisons of the scores obtained under standard and accommodated conditions. We conclude that this research design is useful for understanding the effects of accommodations and does provide evidence of differential group performance, but we also conclude that it does not directly address the validity of inferences made from accommodated assessments.

In the committee's judgment, additional types of validity evidence should be collected. Validation studies in which evidence of criterion relatedness is collected have been conducted with the ACT and the SAT; similar studies should be conducted for NAEP and state assessments as well. We acknowledge that identification of appropriate criterion variables is more straightforward in the context of college admissions than in the K-12 context; however, we encourage efforts to identify and obtain reliable data on concurrent measures that can provide evidence of criterion validity for K-12 achievement results, such as grades, teacher ratings, or scores on other assessments of similar constructs. In addition, analyses of test content and test-takers' cognitive processes would provide further insight into the validity of results from accommodated administrations in the K-12 context. We note that NAEP's sponsors have initiated several studies of this kind since our committee began its investigations, and we encourage them to continue in this vein. Specifically, the committee makes the following recommendation:

Recommendation 5-1: Research should be conducted that focuses on the validation of inferences based on accommodated assessments of students with disabilities and English language learners. Further research should be guided by a conceptual argument about the way accommodations are intended to function and the inferences the test results are intended to support. This research should include a variety of approaches and types of evidence, such as analyses of test content, test-takers' cognitive processes, and criterion-related evidence, and other studies deemed appropriate.

THE VALIDITY OF INFERENCES REGARDING ACCOMMODATED ASSESSMENTS

In an evaluation of a testing program's policies regarding the accommodation of students with disabilities and English language learners, the validity of interpretations of the results should be the primary consideration. A test administered with an accommodation is intended to yield results that are equivalent to the results of a standard administration of the test to a student who has no disability and is fluent in English. However, accommodations can have unintended consequences.

For example, an accommodation might not only allow the student to demonstrate his or her proficiency with regard to the construct being assessed but might also provide that student with an unwarranted advantage over other test-takers. In this case, the resulting score would be an inflated estimate, and hence a less valid indicator, of the test-taker's proficiency.

Thus, determining which accommodation is right for particular circumstances is difficult. The accommodation must at the same time be directly related to the disability or lack of fluency for which it is to compensate and be independent of the constructs on which the student is to be tested. The appropriateness of accommodations might best be understood in terms of a conceptual framework that encompasses both the inferences a test score is designed to support (e.g., the test-taker reads at a particular skill level) and alternative inferences (e.g., the test-taker could not complete the work in the allotted time because of a disability unrelated to his or her skill level on the construct being assessed) that might actually account for the score and therefore impede the collection of the desired information about the test-taker.

Thus the validity of inferences made from the results of any accommodated assessment must be evaluated in terms of the general validation argument for the assessment. That is, there should be a clear definition of the construct the assessment is designed to measure (the targeted skills and knowledge) and the ancillary skills required to demonstrate proficiency on the targeted construct (such as the reading level required to decode the instructions and word problems on an assessment of mathematics skills). Furthermore, the inferences that test designers intend the test results to support should be specified, and evidence in support of claims about how the test results are to be interpreted should be provided.

When accommodations operate as intended, the same kinds of inferences can be drawn from accommodated results as from results based on standard administrations. Only when validation arguments are clearly articulated can the validity of results from accommodated assessments be evaluated. For this reason, the committee examined the available documentation of the constructs to be assessed and the validity evidence laid out for NAEP assessments.

The committee concludes that the validation argument for NAEP in general is not as well articulated as it should be. NAEP officials have not explicitly described the kinds of inferences they believe their data should support, and we found insufficient evidence to support the validity of inferences made from accommodated NAEP scores. While arguments in support of the validity of accommodated administrations of NAEP are discussed in some NAEP materials, more extensive and systematic investigation of the validity of inferences made from these scores is needed. At the same time, as has been noted, existing research does not provide definitive evidence about which procedures will, in general, produce the most valid estimates of performance for students with disabilities and English language learners.

The committee presents a model for evaluating the validity of inferences made from accommodated assessments, based in part on the evidence-centered design approach that has been developed by Hansen, Mislevy, and Steinberg (Hansen and Steinberg, 2004; Hansen et al., 2003; see also Mislevy et al., 2003). This model offers a means of disentangling the potential explanations for observed performance on an assessment and using this analysis to discern the effects of accommodations on the validity of inferences to be based on the observed performance. This approach provides a first step in laying out validity arguments to be investigated through empirical research.

We make three recommendations regarding validity research on accommodations. Although these recommendations are specific to NAEP, we strongly urge the sponsors of state and other large-scale assessment programs to consider them as well.

Recommendation 6-1: NAEP officials should identify the inferences that they intend should be made from its assessment results and clearly articulate the validation arguments in support of those inferences.

Recommendation 6-2: NAEP officials should embark on a research agenda that is guided by the claims and counterclaims for intended uses of results in the validation argument they have articulated. This research should apply a variety of approaches and types of evidence, such as analyses of test content, test-takers' cognitive processes, criterion-related evidence, and other studies deemed appropriate.

Recommendation 6-3: NAEP officials should conduct empirical research to specifically evaluate the extent to which the validation argument that underlies each NAEP assessment and the inferences the assessment was designed to support are affected by the use of particular accommodations.

CONCLUSION

The difficulties related to assessing students with disabilities and English language learners are not new, but the consequences of relying on scores whose accuracy cannot be ensured have become even greater because of the provisions of the No Child Left Behind Act of 2001. Under that legislation, states are responsible for tracking the academic progress of the students with disabilities and English language learners in every school. The consequences for a school of failing to ensure that these students make progress every year toward ambitious targets of performance are serious. However, regardless of that legislation or any modifications that may be made to it, the validity of test-based inferences made about the performance of students with disabilities and English language learners will be critical for those who seek to understand the academic progress of these students, as well as for those who make policies that affect them.

Under the present circumstances, the need for tests results in which users can have justifiable confidence is, if not more critical, at least more immediate. The No Child Left Behind Act requires schools and jurisdictions to take their legal obligations to assess English language learners and students with disabilities more seriously than many have done in the past. While the committee considers this renewed attention to the needs of both groups of students an important development in the effort to close persistent achievement gaps, the goal cannot be met without accurate data. Credible assessment results can play a crucial role in revealing not only where schools are failing these students, but also where they are succeeding with them. Thus it is essential that evidence of the validity of assessment results be thoroughly investigated to be sure that these results can provide useful information regarding students with disabilities and English language learners for schools, local jurisdictions, and the nation.

1

Introduction

Of the nearly 46 million students enrolled in grades K-12 in U.S. public schools during the 2000-2001 school year, some 11.5 percent or nearly 5.5 million were classified as having some kind of disability (U.S. Department of Education, 2002). In addition, nearly 4.6 million or 9.6 percent were identified as English language learners (National Clearinghouse for English Language Acquisition & Language Instruction Educational Programs, 2004). The educational needs of these students vary considerably, as do the strategies for meeting them that are in place in school districts around the country.

The past several decades have seen a significant increase both in the numbers of such students enrolled in U.S. public schools and in attention to their needs, as well as a corresponding demand for information about their academic progress. Agreement has been growing that educational assessments should, whenever possible, include students with disabilities and English language learners so that data can be collected about their progress in school. Legislation has also made their inclusion mandatory. While these two groups of students are often discussed together, it is important to note that the differences between them have important implications in the context of assessment issues. Nevertheless, many of the assessment issues that arise for these two groups of students are similar, and we have addressed them together in this report.

To meet the need to include students from these populations, accommodations are increasingly being used in large-scale assessments, both state assessments and the National Assessment of Educational Progress (NAEP). Drawing on the definition provided in the APA/AERA/NCME *Standards for Educational and Psychological Testing* (American Educational Research Association et al., 1999,

p. 101), we define an accommodation as the general term for any action taken in response to a determination that an individual's disability or lack of English language proficiency requires a departure from established testing protocol. An accommodation may involve a change in the characteristics of specific assessment tasks (e.g., simplified language, native language translation, large font, Braille) or in administrative procedures (e.g., additional time, oral reading of instructions, access to specific equipment). More detailed discussions of accommodations for students with disabilities and English language learners and issues related to their use appear later in the report.

Although the definition is relatively straightforward, identifying students to be included, determining which accommodations are appropriate, and ensuring that scores from accommodated assessments can be interpreted in the same way as scores from regular assessments turn out to be highly complex and problematic issues. To a degree that may surprise those who have not considered the question, the procedures for including both of these groups of students in testing, as well as for providing them with testing accommodations, are far from uniform around the country. Furthermore, research on the effects of various accommodations on performance, as well as on the validity of the inferences made on the basis of scores from accommodated assessments, is inconclusive.

It was in this context that, in 1996, the National Assessment Governing Board (NAGB) and the National Center for Education Statistics (NCES), the groups responsible for developing and implementing policy for NAEP, revised NAEP's policies for including students with disabilities and English language learners in the assessment. They made the changes, the primary effect of which was to include more students in testing, in recognition of changing regulations regarding the testing of these two groups and because of increased appreciation of the value of testing these students. NAEP's sponsors were guided by the importance of maintaining the integrity of NAEP data despite these policy changes, as well as by the importance of keeping NAEP's policies and procedures in accord with those used in other large-scale testing programs administered by states.

In brief, the new policies call for the inclusion of most students with disabilities and most students who have been designated as limited English proficient, and for the exclusion, in general, only of those who cannot meaningfully participate with accommodations approved for NAEP. Under the old policies, far fewer students in these two categories had been included in testing.

We note here that several terms are used to refer to students who are not yet fluent in English, and these may reflect somewhat different understandings of these students and their needs. Although NAEP materials currently use the term LEP (limited English proficient), the committee prefers the more widely used term English language learners, which emphasizes these students' developing English proficiency rather than their limitations.

Two significant challenges faced NAEP's sponsors as they revised their policies and procedures. First, the policies and procedures used by states, districts, and schools vary with respect to which students are classified as having disabilities and being English language learners. These variations in policies and procedures affect decisions about (1) who is included in the assessment, (2) who receives accommodations, (3) what accommodations are allowed and provided, and (4) which students' scores are included in reports. The second major challenge lay in the lack of clear guidance from the available research base regarding the effects of accommodations on test performance. While a considerable body of research exists, findings from these studies are both inconsistent and generally inconclusive (Sireci et al., 2003). The available research is discussed in Chapter 5.

POLICY AND PRACTICE REGARDING
INCLUSION AND ACCOMMODATION

The variation in state policies for handling the assessment of students with disabilities and English language learners is particularly relevant for NAEP. NAEP officials identify the sample of students to be included in the assessment at each participating school, but they must rely on school-level staff to make the decisions about which of the selected students can meaningfully participate and which cannot. That is, selected students whom the local education agency has classified as students with disabilities or English language learners may be excluded from NAEP if school-level staff judge that they cannot meaningfully participate or if they require testing accommodations that NAEP does not permit.[1] It is therefore the local education agency that makes the ultimate decisions about which students will participate in NAEP and which accommodations they may be given, using the guidelines provided by NAEP officials combined with their knowledge of the students.

Students are selected to participate in NAEP on the basis of a complex sampling scheme designed to ensure that a nationally representative subset of students is assessed. Variability in state, district, and school policies and procedures for determining which students are considered to have disabilities or to be English language learners, which of these students can meaningfully be assessed, and which accommodations they will receive, all affect the outcome of the sampling.

This variability has implications for the interpretation of NAEP results. First, local decisions about which students will be included will affect the specific samples that are obtained. Second, the accommodations with which students are

---

[1]Note that according to NAEP policy, English language learners will be included in the assessment without the need for a judgment by school staff if they have received reading and mathematics instruction for three years or more.

provided will affect the conditions under which scores are obtained. As a consequence, a given state's results are affected by these locally made decisions, which may be based on criteria that vary from school to school within a state. Third, national NAEP results, in which scores are aggregated across states, are also affected by these locally made decisions. Finally, a key objective for NAEP is to characterize the achievement of the school-age population in the United States, yet the extent to which NAEP results are representative of the entire population depends on these locally made decisions.

EFFECTS OF ACCOMMODATIONS ON PERFORMANCE AND ON THE INTERPRETATION OF SCORES

The interpretation of NAEP results is further complicated by the fact that the effects of accommodations on test performance are not well understood. Although considerable research has been conducted, a number of questions remain:

- Do commonly used accommodations yield scores that are comparable to those obtained when accommodations are not used? Do they over- or undercorrect for the impediment for which they are designed to compensate?
- Do commonly used accommodations alter the construct being tested?
- What methods should be used for evaluating the effects of a particular accommodation on the validity of test results?

Research on the effects of accommodations has been conducted in different ways, and some of it has yielded intriguing results. The committee commissioned a critical review of this literature, which is discussed in greater detail in Chapter 5. From that review as well as its own observations, the committee notes that research premises and methodologies have varied, stark differences among researchers remain, and little consensus has emerged.

Many researchers, for example, have focused on comparisons of score gains associated with taking the assessment under standard and accommodated conditions. Many studies use a quasi-experimental design in which the target group (e.g., students with disabilities or English language learners) and the comparison group (e.g., nondisabled students or native English speakers) take an assessment with and without accommodations. If scores increase under the accommodated condition for the target group but not for the comparison group, the accommodation is considered to be working as intended.

Other researchers (National Research Council, 2002a, pp. 74-75) have challenged the underlying premise of this research design—that is, they do not agree that such results constitute adequate evidence that an accommodation is working as intended. These critics argue that there may be a confound between the construct being evaluated and the accommodation. Performance on the construct may depend on skills other than those the assessment is intended to measure.

Accommodations may assist all examinees with these skills and consequently help general education students as well as those with identified special needs. These critics argue for different ways of evaluating accommodations, and the committee agrees that alternative methodologies should be used. This point is addressed in greater detail in Chapters 5 and 6.

These questions about the validity of interpretations of accommodated scores are of considerable importance for NAEP, and they are equally important for state assessment programs. At the program level, all large-scale testing programs must develop policies about which accommodations should be allowed and which should not be allowed, given the content and skills being assessed. Likewise, at the individual level, educators must determine which accommodations are appropriate given an individual's needs and the content and skills to be assessed. These decisions should be guided by a clear statement about the inferences to be based on the particular test results and by research findings. In our judgment the available research has not yet yielded the guidance needed to make these decisions; goals for this research are addressed in Chapters 5 and 6.

THE COMMITTEE'S APPROACH

The Board on Testing and Assessment of the National Research Council has for some time been concerned about the issues surrounding the inclusion of students with disabilities and English language learners in large-scale assessments and the effects of accommodations on test performance and the interpretation of scores. In November 2001 the board held a workshop on reporting and interpreting test results for students with disabilities and English language learners who receive test accommodations. That workshop, which was designed to investigate the implications of NAEP's policies regarding the reporting of results for these two groups, made clear that a more comprehensive look at both the variability in inclusion and accommodation policies, and the available research into the effects of accommodations was urgently needed (National Research Council, 2002a).

Thus the National Research Council convened the Committee on Participation of English Language Learners and Students with Disabilities in NAEP and Other Large-Scale Assessments to study these issues. The committee was asked to build on the information learned at the November 2001 workshop (National Research Council, 2002a) and other earlier work in this area (e.g., National Research Council, 1997a, 1997b, 1999a, 1999b, 2000a, 2000b, 2002a). The committee had two primary objectives: (1) to identify what is known about how inclusion and accommodation decisions are currently made and (2) to synthesize recent research about the effects of accommodations on academic test performance and the interpretation of scores. The 2001 workshop included discussions and presentations about states' and NAEP's policies for making inclusion and participation decisions as well as presentations by several individuals who have conducted extensive research in this area (e.g., Jamal Abedi, Stephen Elliott, Laura Hamilton, John Mazzeo, and Gerald Tindal). The workshop report presented summaries of the studies discussed by these authors. In preparation for the committee's work, a critical review of the literature, focusing on studies conducted between January 1990 and December 2002, was commissioned that was intended to build on and extend the research summaries in the workshop report. The authors of the review were Stephen Sireci, associate professor of education and co-director for the center for educational assessment, Stanley Scarpati, associate professor of special education, and Shuhong Li, graduate student in research and evaluation methods, all with the University of Massachusetts at Amherst. This review and critique of the literature assisted the committee with its review and synthesis of research findings. In meeting both aspects of their charge, the committee draws conclusions and makes recommendations about the implications of this information for NAEP policies and the interpretation of NAEP data, as well as for the policies of state assessment programs and the interpretation of their data.

The committee collected information about these issues in several ways. It held two meetings at which presentations were made by a variety of experts. At the first, which focused on policies and procedures, Martha Thurlow of the National Center on Education Outcomes and Charlene Rivera of the Center for Equity and Excellence in Education at George Washington University made presentations on state policies regarding students with disabilities and English language learners, respectively. John Olson of the Council of Chief State School Officers (CCSSO) presented data collected by CCSSO on state policies. Arnold Goldstein of NCES and Jim Carlson of NAGB discussed NAEP policies on accommodation and research conducted on the effects of accommodations on NAEP results. Also at that meeting Stephen Sireci presented the literature review he and his colleagues had conducted (see Sireci et al., 2003) and received feedback from the committee, which was used in preparing the final version of the paper.

At a second meeting, the committee focused on relevant research into the validity of accommodated assessment results. Mary Crovo of NAGB made a presentation about constructs assessed on NAEP reading and mathematics assessments. Eric Hansen of Educational Testing Service presented a second paper prepared for the committee on his plan for an "evidence-centered design approach" to determining allowable accommodations. The committee also heard presentations by Wayne Camara of the College Board and Robert Ziomek of ACT, Inc., on studies of the effects of accommodations on other large-scale assessments (the ACT and the SAT) and on the sampling methodology for students with disabilities and English language learners in NAEP. We reviewed materials made available by NAGB regarding inclusion and accommodation policies and procedures and reports on the participation of students with disabilities and English language learners in the assessment. While the report writing process was under way, several new NAEP reports became available, and we note their relevance to some of our recommendations.

This report of the committee's findings is designed to be of use not only to those who develop policies for NAEP, administer it, or use its results, but also to others interested in the data that large-scale testing can provide about the performance of two groups of students whose educational needs are gaining increased recognition. The committee hopes that this report will be useful for NAGB as it strives to make NAEP more inclusive of students with special needs and to provide results that are more representative of the entire population of school-age children in the United States.

The committee also intends for the report to be useful to states, districts, and schools as they attempt to comply with the terms of the No Child Left Behind Act of 2001. This legislation mandates that states include all students in statewide accountability programs and that they disaggregate assessment results for students with disabilities and English language learners. It holds states accountable for demonstrating that students in these groups are making continuous academic progress. The legislation places considerable demands on state and local testing programs to produce a far greater volume of data than they have previously; because such serious decisions are to be based on test results, the importance of their reliability and validity is greater than ever. Understanding how both inclusion and accommodation decisions are implemented at the local level, as well as the effects of accommodations on test performance, will be key to understanding the meaning of test results for these groups of students.

GUIDE TO THE REPORT

The structure of the report corresponds to the two aspects of the committee's charge. We first deal with the questions of which students are included in testing and the ways in which they are tested. We describe policies, procedures, and practices for identifying, classifying, and including students with disabilities and English language learners, as well as the kinds of accommodations these students are offered. We then address the meaning of scores from accommodated assessments, including what is known about the effects of accommodations on performance in large-scale assessments and the nature of validation arguments and the kinds of evidence that are needed to support inferences made from scores.

Chapter 2 provides background information on students with disabilities and English language learners, on NAEP and other large-scale assessments, and on the issues surrounding the inclusion of these students in testing and the accommodations they need. Chapter 3 discusses the impact of policies currently followed with regard to both including and accommodating these students. Chapter 4 discusses the sampling procedures that are the basis for all NAEP reports on the performance of students with disabilities and English language learners and the factors that complicate the sampling of these groups. Chapter 5 describes the available research on the ways in which the validity of inferences based on test results is affected by accommodations and provides a recommendation for further research in this area. Chapter 6 discusses the kinds of validation arguments that should be articulated for NAEP and for other large-scale assessments. Chapter 7 provides an overview of the primary implications of the committee's findings and recommendations both for NAEP and for the states. The committee's findings and recommendations are presented at the end of the chapters that discuss the evidence on which they are based.

2

Characteristics of the Students, the Assessments, and Commonly Used Accommodations

There are important educational, social, and practical reasons for including both students with disabilities and English language learners in educational assessments whenever possible. There are also laws requiring that these students be included in many kinds of testing, and these laws in many cases provide some guidance for determining how and when these students are to be tested. With more than 20 percent of the students enrolled in public schools in grades K through 12 identified as belonging to one or both of these groups (U.S. Department of Education, 2002; http://www.ncela.gwu.edu/askncela/01leps.htm), the nation clearly has an interest in monitoring their academic progress.

A series of legal mandates, beginning in the 1960s, has spelled out the responsibilities of the nation and the states not only to educate these students and to address their specific needs, but also to collect data regarding many aspects of their schooling and achievement. This chapter provides an overview of the characteristics of each of these groups of students; the legal requirements that affect their participation in educational testing; the large-scale assessments, including the National Assessment of Educational Progress (NAEP), that are used to collect information about their academic progress; and the accommodations that are used in testing these students. This report addresses both students with disabilities and English language learners because members of both groups need accommodations and because many data collection issues have similar implications for both. However, the committee recognizes that the needs and characteristics of these two groups are in many ways very different; where relevant, we have attempted to identify the differences.

THE STUDENTS

Students with Disabilities

According to data collected for the 2000-2001 school year, students with disabilities who are ages 6 through 17 constitute 11.5 percent of the total student enrollment for prekindergarten through 12th grade (U.S. Department of Education, 2002, p. II-19). This percentage accounts for nearly 5.5 million children, the majority of whom are educated in the public school setting, rather than in schools devoted exclusively to serving students with disabilities. States report disability data in 13 categories. Table 2-1 provides information on the percentages of students in each of the categories enrolled in schools in the United States and outlying areas (American Samoa, Guam, Northern Marianas, Puerto Rico, Virgin Islands).

Students with disabilities who qualify for special education are covered by the Individuals with Disabilities Education Act (IDEA). Under this law, these students must be provided with an individualized education plan (IEP), which spells out the goals for each student's instruction and the kinds of services he or she needs, including the accommodations the student requires for standardized assessments. The student's education must, by law, be tailored to his or her

TABLE 2-1 Number and Percentage of All Students with Disabilities Ages 6 Through 17 Served Under the Individuals with Disabilities Education Act During the 2000-2001 School Year

Disability	Number	Percentage
Specific learning disabilities	2,748,569	50.0
Speech or language impairment	1,088,863	19.8
Mental retardation	545,465	9.9
Emotional disabilities	448,310	8.2
Multiple disabilities	106,926	1.9
Hearing impairments	66,092	1.2
Orthopedic impairments	68,253	1.2
Other health impairments	282,470	5.1
Visual impairments	24,033	0.4
Autism	74,166	1.3
Deaf-blindness	1,087	0.0
Traumatic brain injury	13,160	0.2
Developmental delay	28,935	0.5
All disabilities	5,496,329	

NOTE: Percentage total does not add up to 100 percent because numbers were rounded.
SOURCE: U.S. Department of Education (2002).

needs, and assessment of that student's academic progress should reflect an understanding of those goals and of what material the student has had an opportunity to learn.

Students who are considered to have a disability but who do not qualify for special education services are covered by regulations in Section 504 of the Rehabilitation Act of 1973 and the Americans with Disabilities Act of 1990. Such students may have temporary physical problems or a disability, such as one that confines them to a wheelchair, that does not call for a special education plan but does make accommodations necessary, or they may suffer from illnesses that have not progressed to the point at which they need special education. Some students with attention deficit disorder receive services under Section 504 regulations rather than through special education. In most states, the Section 504 Plan specifies the accommodations the student requires for standardized testing. Both IDEA and Section 504 regulations prohibit discrimination on the basis of a disability and therefore require that students who need testing accommodations be provided with them.

The characteristics of the students who are classified as having a disability are extremely diverse and tend to vary along a continuum rather than manifesting themselves in tidy categories. Moreover, factors such as the nature of the special services that are available in the jurisdiction, the characteristics of the general education classrooms in the jurisdiction, as well as social and interpersonal factors, can affect the diagnosis of students' needs.

An earlier National Research Council committee (National Research Council, 1997a) noted specifically that the extent to which a child's performance in school can be explained by intrinsic characteristics of the child, rather than the characteristics of the context in which that child is being educated, is difficult to discern. Commenting on the diversity of students with disabilities as a group, that committee further noted that they can meaningfully be described as a group only in the context of the rights they are accorded under the IDEA and other legislation (National Research Council, 1997a). This diversity complicates attempts to make generalizations about students with disabilities as a group, an issue we address in greater detail later in this report. This chapter also describes the IDEA and the other legislation that affects the education of these students. Additional detail about the process of identifying students with disabilities and determining appropriate accommodations for them appears in Chapter 4.

English Language Learners

Nearly 4.6 million students in U.S. public schools were designated English language learners during the 2000-2001 school year (http://www.ncela.gwu.edu/askncela/01leps.htm). This group of students is generally understood to include all those whose language skills in English are in need of development if they are to demonstrate their full academic potential. The total number of students reported by states to be English language learners has nearly doubled during the past decade (Kindler, 2002). That growth has not been evenly distributed among the states, however. California, Florida, Texas, and New York, for example, have the largest numbers of English language learners, and have all seen growth in this group of students in the period from 1997-1998 to 2000-2001, but other states—which started out with smaller numbers—have seen more dramatic growth in that period. Georgia, for example, experienced a 113 percent increase in the number of enrolled students classified as English language learners. Other states have seen sizeable, though somewhat smaller, increases, including Mississippi with a 79 percent increase, Indiana with a 32 percent increase, Wisconsin with a 30 percent increase, North Carolina with a 27 percent increase, Ohio with an 18 percent increase, and Maryland with a 15 percent increase. A few states, most notably New Mexico, lost English language learners during that period (Kindler, 2002).

Although the majority of English language learners are native Spanish speakers, states reported enrolling students who spoke more than 400 languages in the 2000-2001 school year. Table 2-2 provides estimates of the numbers of English language learners who report various languages as their first, or native language (http://www.ncela.gwu.edu/askncela/05toplangs.htm).

As a group, English language learners bring with them to U.S. schools a diverse range of both English-language skills and previous academic experience. Some are fully literate in their native languages and ready to plunge into content appropriate to their age and grade level. Others are not, bringing very different needs to their classrooms. These students vary in terms of how long they have lived in the United States, how much exposure they have had to English in their previous schooling, the age at which they entered U.S. schools, the number of years they have been classified as English language learners and the nature of supports they may already have received, their prior academic performance, and socioeconomic characteristics (National Research Council, 1997b). Thus, as with students with disabilities, it is important to recognize that English language learners are not a uniform group.

There is no federal legislation that lays out regulations and procedures for the education of English language learners in the way that the IDEA does for students with disabilities. Hence, both the means by which English language learners are identified and the services they are offered through the public schools vary considerably across jurisdictions. To determine which students need English instruction or other linguistic support in addition to their regular academic work, most states either use a test (commercially available assessments or assessments developed at the district level) or simply make informal evaluations of students' ability to function and succeed in classrooms in which instruction is offered in English. However, in determining whether or not to include students in large-scale achievement testing programs, most states focus on the number of years students have been in the United States or the number of years students have been receiving

TABLE 2-2 Most Common Language Groups for English Language Learners

Language	Estimated Number	Estimated Percentage
Spanish	3,598,451	79.00
Vietnamese	88,906	2.00
Hmong	70,768	1.60
Chinese, Cantonese	46,466	1.00
Korean	43,969	1.00
Haitian Creole	42,236	0.90
Arabic	41,279	0.90
Russian	37,157	0.80
Tagalog	34,133	0.70
Navajo	27,029	0.60
Khmer	26,815	0.60
Chinese, Mandarin	22,374	0.50
Portuguese	20,787	0.50
Urdu	18,649	0.40
Serbo-Croatian	17,163	0.40
Lao	15,549	0.30
Japanese	15,453	0.30
Chuukese	15,194	0.30
Chinese, unspecified	14,817	0.30
Chamorro	14,354	0.30
Marshallese	13,808	0.30
Punjabi	13,200	0.30
Armenian	13,044	0.30
Polish	11,847	0.30
French	11,328	0.20
Hindi	10,697	0.20
Native American, unspecified	10,174	0.20
Ukrainian	9,746	0.20
Pohnpeian	9,718	0.20
Farsi	9,670	0.20
Somali	9,230	0.20
Cherokee	9,229	0.20
Gujarati	7,943	0.20
Albanian	7,874	0.20
German	7,705	0.20
Yup'ik	7,678	0.20
Bengali	6,587	0.10
Romanian	5,898	0.10
Ilocano	5,770	0.10
Other languages	152,082	3.50
Total	4,544,777	

NOTE: Percentage total does not add up to 100 percent because numbers were rounded.
SOURCE: Available: http://www.ncela.gwu.edu/askncela/05toplangs.htm.

linguistic support services (Council of Chief State School Officers, 2002). In Chapters 3 and 4, state policies regarding the inclusion of English language learners in large-scale testing programs and the provision of appropriate testing accommodations for them are discussed in greater detail.

LEGAL REQUIREMENTS

The rights of students with disabilities and English language learners are covered by a complex maze of federal laws. The Fourteenth Amendment to the U.S. Constitution provides the basis for much of the legislation concerning disadvantaged students' rights to education. It guarantees protection from discrimination and provides for due process. Public schools are thus prohibited from denying students equal protection of the law or life, liberty, or property interests without due process. Title VI of the Civil Rights Act of 1964 prohibits discrimination on the basis of race, color, or national origin and has been interpreted as "requiring the inclusion of English language learners in testing" (Coleman in National Research Council, 2002a, p. 14). The reasoning behind this interpretation is that participation in testing is a benefit; categorically excluding a student from testing amounts to denying him or her a benefit, and it has the potential consequence of severely limiting that student's future educational opportunities.

The first piece of legislation to specifically address the educational needs of these groups was the Elementary and Secondary Education Act (ESEA) of 1965, which explicitly required that disadvantaged students be held by states to the same high standards that applied to other students (Taylor in National Research Council, 2000b, p. 14). Title I of this legislation, which has been renewed and modified numerous times since the 1960s, has called for these students to be assessed "appropriately" and for proper accommodations to be used to achieve this accountability. States must abide by these requirements in order to receive federal Title I funding, which is provided to support the education of disadvantaged children.

Since the original passage of the ESEA, a number of other federal laws that relate to the testing of English language learners and students with disabilities have been passed, and they fall into two categories: laws that deal with fundamental student rights and laws that are related to a particular federal grant program. Laws in the first category provide that students who are in public or private schools that are recipients of federal funds are protected by guarantees related to appropriate test use provisions.[1]

The other category of laws, those that relate to federal grant programs, oper-

---

[1]Such laws include the Fourteenth Amendment, Title VI of the Civil Rights Act of 1964, the Equal Educational Opportunities Act, Section 504 of the 1973 Rehabilitation Act, and Title II of the Americans with Disabilities Act of 1990.

ate somewhat differently. They have very specific requirements that do not give students rights to file legal claims, but instead set conditions for the award and use of federal funds around certain specified test use practices.[2] The Individuals with Disabilities Education Act (P.L. 105-12) falls into the category of a grants program, since it provides funds to states to serve students with disabilities, but it is also a civil rights law that extends the constitutional right to equality of educational opportunity to students with disabilities who need special education. The laws that specifically affect each of the two groups that are the subject of this report are discussed in greater detail below.

Students with Disabilities

Individuals with Disabilities Education Act[3]

The IDEA is the primary federal law providing funding and policy guidance for the education of students with disabilities; its major policy goals have remained constant since the IDEA's predecessor, P.L. 94-142, was enacted in 1975. The IDEA provides funds to states to serve students with disabilities who are in need of special education on the condition that the states ensure an appropriate education for them. As noted above, the IDEA is also a civil rights law extending the constitutional right to equality of educational opportunity to students with disabilities needing special education. The law sets out three basic requirements with which states and local districts must comply:

- All children who have disabilities and are in need of special education must be provided a free, appropriate public education.
- Each child's education must be determined on an individualized basis and designed to meet his or her unique needs in the least restrictive environment.
- The rights of children and their families must be ensured and protected through procedural safeguards.

The primary mechanism for ensuring that the educational objectives of the IDEA are met is the individualized education program (IEP), which must be prepared for each child identified as having a disability and being in need of special education. The IEP is a written statement that describes the child's current

---

[2]Laws that fall into this category are Titles I and VII of the 1994 ESEA, the Goals 2000: Educate America Act, and the No Child Left Behind Act. Title I of the 1994 ESEA serves disadvantaged, high-poverty students, while Title VII serves language-minority students. As noted above, Goals 2000 and No Child Left Behind promote standards-based reform efforts.

[3]Text is adapted from National Research Council (1997a, pp. 46-47).

level of educational performance; the annual goals and short-term objectives that have been established for him or her; the specific educational and related support services to be provided, including instructional and testing accommodations; and procedures for evaluating progress on the stated goals and objectives. The centerpiece of the law is Part B, which authorizes grants to states to support the education of students with disabilities and outlines the requirements that states and districts must meet as a condition of that funding.

Section 504 of the Rehabilitation Act of 1973[4]

Because the IDEA is essentially a federal grants program, state participation is voluntary and the act's requirements are imposed on states and local districts only if they choose to accept the funding. All states are currently accepting IDEA funding. However, even without the IDEA, school districts would still have a legal obligation to serve students with disabilities because of two federal civil rights statutes: Section 504 of the Rehabilitation Act of 1973 and the Americans with Disabilities Act of 1990 (ADA).

Section 504 prohibits discrimination solely on the basis of disability against persons who are otherwise qualified in federally assisted programs and activities. It applies to virtually all public schools, since the overwhelming majority receive some form of federal assistance. In the context of elementary and secondary education, Section 504 regulations require that local districts provide a free, appropriate public education to each school-age child, regardless of the nature or severity of the person's disability.

Whereas the IDEA addresses individuals with disabilities who need special education, Section 504 defines and protects a broader category of these individuals, whether or not they require special education programs or related services. So, for example, elementary and secondary students requiring only special accommodations but not special education are covered by Section 504. Section 504 requires the provision of reasonable accommodations for individuals with disabilities who are otherwise qualified to participate in an educational program or activity.

Americans with Disabilities Act[5]

The Americans with Disabilities Act of 1990 is a comprehensive federal civil rights statute that provides a "national mandate to end discrimination against individuals with disabilities in private-sector employment, all public services and public accommodations, transportation, and telecommunications" (Hardman et

---

[4]Text is adapted from National Research Council (1997a, pp. 47-50).
[5]Text is adapted from National Research Council (1997b, pp. 50-51).

al., 1996, p. 13). The ADA also requires "reasonable accommodations," a term that is being interpreted through case law. Perhaps the greatest impact of the ADA on the education of students with disabilities has been the increase in the availability of accommodations for persons in the private sector in employment, recreation, living arrangements, and mobility, which has led to a more comprehensive effort to prepare children with disabilities for greater adult participation in community settings.

The ADA's Title II mirrors the nondiscrimination provisions of Section 504. It extends civil rights protections for otherwise qualified persons with disabilities to include services, programs, and activities provided by "public entities," which include state and local governments and their instrumentalities. Because of this provision, access to state and local programs must be provided regardless of whether the states receive federal funding. Thus, even public schools not covered by other federal laws governing special education must comply with the ADA.

State Laws

In addition to the federal laws governing the education of students with disabilities, all states and many local governments have enacted statutes and regulations designed to promote the rights of students with disabilities. Since states must have a plan in order to qualify for IDEA funds, all have enacted special education statutes that incorporate the major provisions of the IDEA. Some state laws, however, extend beyond the federal criteria for an appropriate education.

The IEP Process[6]

The provisions of the federal IDEA and Section 504 and the requirements of most state special education laws require an individualized, appropriate education for students with disabilities. Two key assumptions about student evaluation and identification underlie these requirements. First, students are not eligible for coverage under the laws unless they have either been identified as being "disabled" and in need of special education or, under Section 504, are either defined as "disabled" or "regarded as being disabled." Consequently, a process is needed to determine whether each individual is eligible for the procedural protections or services each law provides. Second, the laws require a process to evaluate each individual with a disability in order to identify the student's capabilities and needs and the appropriate programs and services.

The development of an IEP is the process that has been devised to meet these needs. In this process, teachers, other service providers, and parents work together

---

[6]Text is adapted from National Research Council (1997a, pp. 56-57).

to define and document the program and services the student needs (Zettel, 1982). The IEP process includes both substantive protections governing a student's educational program and procedural requirements that both foster the participation of parents in educational planning and provide an independent review mechanism if disputes arise between educators and the family over how or where to educate the student.

Case Law

The IDEA, Section 504, and the ADA are being further clarified through case law. Several recent cases, which are class action suits brought against states in which students were denied the accommodations specified in their IEPs, are relevant to this report. In Indiana (*Rene v. Reed*, 751 N.E.2d 736, Ind. Ct. App. 2001), a decision was rendered by the state appellate court that accommodations specified in an IEP need not be provided in a state assessment if they would affect the validity of test results. However, in a similar case in Oregon, state officials agreed to a settlement in which the state assumes the burden of proof for demonstrating the inappropriateness of an accommodation (*Advocates for Special Kids (ASK) v. Oregon State Board of Education*, Federal District Court, No. CV99-263 K1). In this case it was established that students with disabilities whose IEPs specify accommodations would receive those accommodations on statewide assessments unless the state of Oregon could prove that the accommodations would alter the construct being measured and thus invalidate the results.

A case in California (*Juleus Chapman et al. v. California Department of Education et al.*, No. C01-1780) was decided along similar lines. This case, which provides the basis for California's policies on accommodations, made a distinction between the question of whether students have the right to take tests with accommodations provided for in their IEP or Section 504 Plans (the ruling affirmed this right), and the question of whether the resulting scores must be treated as equivalent to those from unaccommodated administrations (the court ruled that they need not be). These cases have brought national attention to the need for empirical evidence to document that certain accommodations are inappropriate for certain types of tests. That is, evidence is needed to evaluate whether providing an accommodation interferes with assessment of the targeted construct. We address this issue in detail in Chapters 5 and 6.

English Language Learners

For English language learners, Titles I and VII of the 1994 Elementary and Secondary Education Act have been key pieces of legislation. These provisions required that states report disaggregated achievement test results for both students with disabilities and English language learners so that the progress of each group could be monitored. Under these laws, school districts have what the law calls an "affirmative obligation" to provide English language learners with equal access to educational programs so that students have the opportunity to become proficient in English and to achieve the high academic standards of their educational programs. School districts must ensure that their curricular and instructional programs for English language learners are recognized as educationally sound or otherwise vouched for as legitimate educational strategies, and that they are implemented effectively and monitored over time (and altered as needed) to ensure success.

The fundamental legal requirement is that the achievement of all English language learners must be assessed as part of state testing programs, and that reasonable accommodations be provided for those who need them. The states are required to identify the languages spoken by students in their school systems and "make every effort to develop" assessments that can be used with these students (National Research Council, 2000b, p. 15). They are required to consider either accommodations or native language testing to obtain scores that are valid for their students, depending on the students' needs and the instruction they have received. These requirements are qualified by the phrase "to the extent practicable" to allow states some leeway in addressing changing populations of nonnative English speakers and other practical concerns.

While some flexibility in strategies is allowed, states are required to apply their policies regarding accommodations consistently across districts and schools. States are required to include all English language learners[7] in assessment programs used for Title I purposes and must make a determination for each student of what form of testing, accommodations, or alternate language testing would yield the most valid and reliable results for that student. The content and performance standards against which English language learners are tested may not be less rigorous than those for other students, and English language learners must be tested at all of the grades included in the statewide testing system.

The Title I legislation builds on the development over several decades of legal standards that have affected the schooling of English language learners, which began with Title VI of the 1964 Civil Rights Act, discussed above. A U.S. Supreme Court case, *Lau v. Nichols* (414 U.S. 563, 94 S. Ct. 786, 1974), later followed up on the principles of educational equality established there, holding that "there is no equality of treatment merely by providing students with the same facilities, textbooks, and curriculum; for students who do not understand English are effectively foreclosed from any meaningful education."

Also in 1974, Congress enacted the Equal Education Opportunities Act, judicial interpretations of which made more explicit what states and school districts must do to enable English language learners to participate "meaningfully" in the educational programs they offer. These standards were used in a 1981

---

[7]The legislation uses the term LEP, limited English proficient, students.

appeals court ruling, *Castaneda v. Pickard* (648 F. 2d 989, 5th Cir. 1981), which articulates basic requirements for programs for children with limited English proficiency. A 1991 policy statement from the Department of Education's Office for Civil Rights explains how the Casteneda case applies to possible violations of Title VI.[8] The policy statement notes that "Title VI does not mandate any particular program for instruction for LEP students," but goes on to say that such programs must be recognized by experts in the field as being sound.

No Child Left Behind Act of 2001

The inclusion of students with disabilities and English language learners in achievement testing programs, as well as the accommodations they would need to participate in testing programs, had thus already been the subject of a significant amount of legislation when the No Child Left Behind Act was passed in 2001. The new law expanded on the requirements already in place in several ways. It requires states, districts, and schools to be held accountable not only for making sure that their students continuously improve on average, but also for making sure that specific groups, including English language learners and students with disabilities, also improve continually. The law calls for annual testing in reading and mathematics at each of grades 3 through 8, and it spells out both targets for improvement and a series of steps to be taken to intervene with schools that fail to meet these targets. States are to define proficiency levels and must bring 100 percent of their students to that level within 12 years.[9] The targets must also be met by disadvantaged students, including students in poverty and racial/ethnic minorities as well as students with disabilities and English language learners.

In addition, the act requires that individual-level results be aggregated to the school level and that school-level results be used to make judgments about adequate yearly progress. Sanctions are levied against schools that do not meet their goals; these are progressively more serious with each year the school fails to meet its targets. It should be noted here that the U.S. Department of Education has reviewed some of the specific provisions of the law in recent months in response to issues that have arisen in implementing it in many states. Most recently the department has modified the policies regarding students with limited English skills (Zehr, 2004).

This new legislation is in the category of laws that stipulate conditions that states must meet in order to maintain their eligibility for federal education funds.

---

[8]The Office for Civil Rights of the U.S. Department of Education is the federal agency charged with enforcement of civil rights law as it pertains to education. Its policy statements describe the legal standards and court precedents that are relevant to particular issues and are designed to assist policy makers and others in adhering to the law.

[9]As noted earlier, states must include no less than 95 percent of students in each subgroup in assessments and must follow the provisions in the IDEA regarding accommodations, guidelines, and alternate assessments (P.L. 107-110, Jan. 8, 2002, 115 STAT 1448-1449).

While the law does not provide detailed guidelines for the testing of students with disabilities or English language learners, its requirements for data, as well as the high stakes it attaches to test results, add additional weight not only to the importance of accurate data but also to the particular challenges of obtaining valid and reliable results for these two groups of students.

PROFESSIONAL MEASUREMENT STANDARDS

In addition to the legal requirements that govern the testing of students with disabilities and English language learners, there are also standards regarding their testing that have been developed by the professional communities involved in educational measurement, psychology, and educational research. Development of the *Standards for Educational and Psychological Testing* (1999) was guided by members of the American Educational Research Association (AERA), the American Psychological Association (APA), and the National Council on Measurement in Education (NCME). These standards, while not legally binding, are a widely respected guide to the best practices that have evolved over several decades. The most recent edition of the *Standards* devotes a chapter to the testing of individuals of diverse language backgrounds and a chapter to the testing of individuals with disabilities. They offer a number of specific guidelines for testing each group; readers are referred to Chapters 9 and 10 of the *Standards* for a detailed discussion of the relevant issues.

LARGE-SCALE ASSESSMENTS

Large-scale assessments are those given to large numbers of students for purposes that include program evaluation, establishing standards or requirements, and matching students to appropriate instructional programs. NAEP, a national assessment that yields the data on which the widely publicized Nation's Report Cards are based, provides data on groups of students so that educational progress across the nation can be monitored. Many other assessments are used every year in states and districts. These assessments have a variety of purposes and use a variety of methods to obtain data.

National Assessment of Educational Progress

As mandated by Congress in 1969, NAEP surveys the educational accomplishments of students in the United States. The assessment monitors changes in achievement in different subject areas, providing a measure of students' learning at critical points in their school experience. Results from the assessment inform national and state policy makers about student performance, assisting them in evaluating the conditions and progress of the nation's education system (http://nces.ed.gov/nationsreportcard/about/).

NAEP includes two distinct assessment programs, referred to as "long-term trend NAEP" (or "trend NAEP") and "main NAEP," with different instrumentation, sampling, administration, and reporting practices. As the name implies, long-term trend NAEP is designed to document changes in academic performance over time, and thus the test items generally remain unchanged. It is administered to nationally representative samples of 9-, 13-, and 17-year-olds. Over the years, trends have been reported in subject areas such as reading, writing, mathematics, and science. For the next decade or so, NAEP's plans call for reporting trends in the areas of reading and mathematics.

By contrast, main NAEP test items reflect current thinking about what students know and can do in the NAEP subject areas. They are based on recently developed content and skill outlines in reading, writing, mathematics, science, U.S. history, world history, geography, civics, the arts, and foreign languages. Main NAEP assessments can take advantage of the latest advances in assessment methodology. Main NAEP results can be used to track short-term changes in performance. Main NAEP has two components: national NAEP and state NAEP.

National NAEP tests nationally representative samples of students enrolled in public and nonpublic schools in grades 4, 8, and 12 in a variety of subject areas (U.S. Department of Education, National Center for Education Statistics and Office of Educational Research and Improvement, 2003). It reports information for the nation and specific geographic regions of the country. State NAEP assessments are administered to representative samples of students enrolled in public schools in the states (U.S. Department of Education, National Center for Education Statistics and Office of Educational Research and Improvement, 2003). State NAEP uses the same large-scale assessment materials as national NAEP. It is administered to grades 4 and 8 in reading, writing, mathematics, and science (although not always in both grades in each of these subjects).

The No Child Left Behind Act of 2001 made participation in state NAEP mandatory and specified requirements for NAEP. Accordingly (http://nces.ed.gov/nationsreportcard/about/assessmentsched.asp):

- NAEP must administer reading and mathematics assessments for grades 4 and 8 every other year in all states.
- In addition, NAEP must test these subjects on a nationally representative basis at grade 12 at least as often as it has done in the past, or every four years.
- Provided funds are available, NAEP may conduct national and state assessments at grades 4, 8, and 12 in additional subject matter, including writing, science, history, geography, civics, economics, foreign languages, and arts.

Until 2002, state and national NAEP were based on separate samples of students. Beginning with the 2002 assessments, a combined sample of schools was selected for both state and national NAEP. It was thought that drawing a subset of schools from all of the state samples to produce national estimates would reduce the testing burden by decreasing the total number of schools participating in state and national NAEP. From this group of schools, representing 50 states, a subsample of students was identified as the national subset. Therefore, the national sample is a subset of the combined sample of students assessed in each participating state (http://nces.ed.gov/nationsreportcard/about/).

NAEP differs fundamentally from many other testing programs in that its objective is to obtain accurate measures of academic achievement for groups of students rather than for individuals. To achieve this goal, NAEP uses complex sampling, scaling, and analysis procedures. NAEP's current practice is to use a scale of 0 to 500 or 0 to 300 to summarize performance on the assessments. NAEP reports scores on this scale in a given subject area for the nation as a whole, for individual states, and for population subsets based on demographic and background characteristics. Results are tabulated over time to provide both long-term and short-term trend information. In addition to providing straightforward scale scores for each group, NAEP uses a process for defining what are called achievement levels as an alternative way of presenting the results. NAGB has established, by policy, definitions for three levels of student achievement: basic, proficient, and advanced (http://www.nagb.org). The achievement levels describe the range of performance that the National Assessment Governing Board believes should be demonstrated at each grade, and it reports the percentage of students at or above each achievement level.

NAEP is intended to serve as a monitor of the educational progress of students in the United States. Although its results receive a fair amount of public attention, they have typically not been used for purposes that have significant consequences for groups or individuals, in part because they do not generate individual or school-level scores. However, a survey has shown that NAEP results are used for a variety of purposes, some of which are beyond those specified in the legislation governing it or envisioned by its developers (DeVito, 1996). These include:

1. describing the status of the education system,
2. describing student performance by demographic group,
3. identifying the knowledge and skills over which students have (or do not have) mastery,
4. supporting judgments about the adequacy of observed performance,
5. arguing the success or failure of instructional content and strategies,
6. discussing relationships between achievement and school and family variables,
7. reinforcing the call for high academic standards and educational reform, and
8. arguing for system and school accountability.

It is important to point out that not all of these uses are aligned with the original objectives for NAEP and that some may not be empirically supportable uses of the data. Chapter 5 discusses in detail the ways in which evidence of the validity of inferences that might be made about test scores can be gathered.

The ways in which NAEP results are used are likely to change as a result of the No Child Left Behind Act. While the law does not make new requirements of NAEP (at one time there was a plan to use NAEP directly as a benchmark for state test results), it does mandate state participation in biennial NAEP assessments of fourth and eighth grade reading and math. It is expected that NAEP will serve as a rough benchmark for each state's assessment results, in the sense that significant discrepancies between a state's scores on its own assessment and on NAEP would signal the need for further investigation of that state's data on student performance (National Assessment Governing Board, 2002a; Taylor, 2002).

State Assessments

As noted, the principal purpose of NAEP is to provide a snapshot of what groups of students across the nation (e.g., fourth graders, Hispanic fourth graders, fourth graders enrolled in urban schools, fourth graders who live in Illinois) have achieved in a variety of subjects. The assessments reflect broad-based consensus as to what are the key elements of each subject that students should be expected to know and be able to do in each tested grade. States and districts have sought similar information about their students' mastery of the material deemed critical in their own standards and have developed state assessments that reflect state-level priorities with regard to subject matter. In addition, although some states use assessments with a structure similar to that of NAEP, states generally have a variety of objectives for their assessments that differ from the objectives for NAEP. In many states, for example, parents and others have consistently demanded that whatever testing their children participate in yield individual scores. Parents and others want the state and district assessments their children must take to tell them not just how well the school or district is doing but also how their own children are doing. For the most part, states and districts test their students in order to gain information for the following purposes:

- Accountability—providing evidence of the performance of teachers, administrators, schools, districts, or states, relative to established standards or benchmarks, or in comparison to others, or both.
- Decisions about students—providing data that are used in making important decisions about individual students, such as placement in academic programs, grade promotion, and graduation.
- Program evaluation—providing evidence of the outcome of a particular educational program in terms of student performance.

- Tracking of long-term trends—providing evidence of changes in the performance of groups of students, such as those enrolled in a particular grade, school, or school district, those belonging to population subgroups, etc.
- Diagnosis—providing information about students' strengths and weaknesses with regard to specific material or skills (such as proficiency in English), for use in improving teaching and learning.

Regardless of the purpose of their assessment programs, states and districts are held accountable for the achievement of all of their students with disabilities and English language learners and thus are required to include them in many of the assessments they use, although attaining that goal has proved challenging. By contrast, however, NAEP has not included all students from these two groups in testing, nor is it currently planning to do so. For practical reasons, NAEP has limited both the kinds of students that can be included and the accommodations that can be offered. While the No Child Left Behind Act of 2001 does not call for direct linking of NAEP results with those of states, this discrepancy in inclusion policies is likely to prove a serious difficulty for a number of reasons. Chapter 3 addresses in greater detail the policies of both NAEP and the assessments used by states with regard to including and accommodating these students, and provides further discussion of the implications of these policies.

ACCOMMODATIONS: ISSUES AND PRACTICE

Many of the laws described earlier make reference to the need for students with disabilities and English language learners to receive appropriate accommodations when they are included in educational assessments. The accommodation should allow the student to demonstrate what he or she knows or can do in spite of his or her disability or limited fluency in English, without providing him or her with any other advantage. Perhaps the most straightforward example is the provision of a Braille version of a written test for a student with visual limitations. However, because the circumstances that can cause a student to need an accommodation when participating in assessments are so varied, the questions surrounding accommodations are frequently far less straightforward than this example.

Consider a student who has a decoding disability that makes it difficult for him or her to respond to word problems on a mathematics assessment. It may take this student so long to decode the instructions and the text in the individual problems that he or she runs out of time before completing all of the items, even though this student's mathematics skills are adequate for the tasks presented. Accommodations provided to a student in this situation may include the opportunity to hear the instructions and text read aloud or the provision of extra testing time. While the decision to provide this accommodation may be relatively straightforward, determining the amount of time that will compensate for the decoding disability without giving the student an additional advantage is much more complicated. Furthermore, the identification of an appropriate accommodation depends on a clear definition of the construct(s) being measured on the assessment. In this example, if the mathematics assessment were intended to measure speed of response, the provision of extra time might interfere with measurement of the targeted construct(s). Issues associated with determining the appropriateness of accommodations are discussed in greater detail in Chapter 6.

The assumption underlying the accommodation is that every student has a true level of competence in each tested subject area, and that a perfectly reliable and valid assessment will reveal that true performance. The accommodation is intended only to compensate for factors that prevent the student from demonstrating his or her true competence, and not to improve his or her performance beyond that level. However, in real-world testing situations, a variety of factors may influence any student's performance on an assessment. There may be factors extraneous to the construct being tested that affect all students, not just those who need accommodation. Students without disabilities, for example, might also find that the time allowed for a test is too short, and their scores may improve if they are allowed extra time to complete their work. The critical questions to be answered are whether the scores from an accommodated assessment are comparable to scores from the unaccommodated assessment, and, furthermore, whether similar inferences can be made from the results of each.

Mechanisms for evaluating the validity of scores from accommodated assessments, as well as research into those questions are discussed in later chapters. Here we explore the specific factors that affect the accommodation of students with disabilities and English language learners.

Accommodations for Students with Disabilities

Now that states are required by law to strive to include all students in their accountability programs, the need for testing accommodations has become even more acute.[10] As was mentioned earlier, the principal guide to assessing students with disabilities is the IEP, developed by a team that includes both school staff and the parent(s) or guardian. In addition to describing the student's current level of performance, defining the educational goals for the student, and describing the supports or services the student will need, the IEP also specifies how the student may participate in state and local assessments and any accommodations that must

---

[10]States are also permitted to offer alternate assessments for some students (P.L. 107-10). Alternate assessments are mostly used for the small minority of students whose curriculum is significantly different from that of general education students and who are held to different sets of standards. Alternate assessments typically will not support the same inferences as the regular assessments or yield comparable results.

be provided for testing. The development of the IEP is guided by legal requirements, and the IEP is considered the authoritative statement of what is appropriate
for the student. There are times when state accommodation policies may be in
direct conflict with the recommendations made in a student's IEP; for example,
the IEP may require that the student receive the read-aloud accommodation on
standardized assessments while the state may not permit that accommodation on
all assessments (e.g., on assessments of reading comprehension). What is done in
that situation varies from state to state; for example, states have various policies
for reporting results of assessments in which accommodations that are not
approved for the assessment were used (National Research Council, 2002a). In
general, the specification of accommodations is to be based on the definition of
the student's needs and is to be consistent with accommodations that are used for
instruction.

There are several issues that can make both determining the appropriateness
of accommodations and evaluating the results of accommodated assessments
difficult. Disabilities can affect test-taking and scores in varying and sometimes
unpredictable ways. For example, a student with a visual impairment may require
a Braille version of a test as an accommodation. However, reading Braille can be
time-intensive, since it is not possible to skim Braille text; thus, unless extra time
is also provided, the student may not be able to demonstrate his or her true
proficiency in the assessed subject area. Another difficulty is that disabilities can
overlap with achievement constructs measured in assessments. For example, a
student whose learning disability is in the area of mathematical computations
may require a calculator as an accommodation. However, when an assessment is
intended to measure computational skills, provision of a calculator would directly
interfere with measurement of the intended construct. Thus both identification of
appropriate accommodations and interpretation of accommodated scores depends
on precise understanding of the nature of the student's disability.

The principal testing accommodations that are offered to students with disabilities are listed by category in Table 2-3.

Accommodations for English Language Learners

The requirements for including English language learners under the No Child
Left Behind Act are, as we have seen, very similar to those for students with
disabilities (although, as noted earlier, some increased flexibility in including
English language learners has recently been written into the requirement).
Although the requirements are similar, the nature of the challenge to educators is
slightly different. First, there is no process like the IEP process that exists for
students with disabilities to guide the diagnosis of students' needs, the determination of how federal and other laws might apply to the individual student, or the
identification of appropriate accommodations for the student.

Nevertheless, English language learners need accommodations because lan-

TABLE 2-3 Testing Accommodations Offered to Students with Disabilities

Setting	Timing
• Individual • Small group • Study carrel • Separate location • Special lighting • Adaptive or special furniture • Special acoustics • Minimal distractions environment	• Extended time • Flexible schedule • Frequent breaks during testing • Frequent breaks on one subtest but not another

Presentation	Response
• Audio tape • Braille edition • Large print • Audio amplification devices, hearing aids • Noise buffers • Prompts on tape • Increased space between items • Fewer items per page • Simplify language in directions • Highlight verbs in instructions by underlining • One complete sentence per line in reading passages • Key words or phrases in directions highlighted • Sign directions to student • Read directions to student • Reread directions for each page of questions • Multiple choice questions followed by answer down side with bubbles to right • Clarify directions • Cues (arrows, stop signs) on answer form • Provide additional examples • Visual magnification devices • Templates to reduce visible print • Eliminate items that cannot be revised and estimate score	• Mark in response booklet • Use of a Brailler • Tape record for later verbatim translation • Use of scribe • Word processor • Communication device • Copying assistance between drafts • Adaptive or special furniture • Dark or heavy raised lines • Pencil grips • Large diameter pencil • Calculator • Abacus • Arithmetic tables • Spelling dictionary • Spell checker • Special acoustics • Paper secured to work area with tape/magnets

Scheduling	Other
• Specific time of day • Subtests in different order • Best time for students • Over several days	• Special test preparation • On-task/focusing prompts • Others that do not fit into other categories

SOURCE: Adapted from Thurlow et al. (2002).

guage barriers have the potential to prevent them from demonstrating what they know and can do in several ways. Regardless of which academic area is being assessed, a test administered in English is, in part, a measure of English language skills (American Psychological Association et al., 1999). While using tests that avoid unnecessarily complex language can enable English language learners to demonstrate their skills with respect to the measured construct, distinguishing academic progress from language skills is difficult (e.g., in mathematics when word problems are used).

Thus, the goal for accommodating English language learners is the same one that guides the accommodation of students with disabilities, that is, to obtain a more valid assessment of their skills with regard to the tested construct than is possible without the accommodation. At the same time, it is important to note that for students whose English proficiency is truly minimal, no accommodation can offer a reasonable adaptation of an assessment that is in English; in such cases, other means must be found to assess students' academic strengths and needs (and the resulting scores are not likely to be comparable to those from the original assessment). Assessments can be translated, but a number of issues arise when this is done because the difficulty level and other characteristics of translated text can be significantly different from those of the original.

The accommodations available for use with English language learners can present difficulties similar to those that arise in accommodating students with disabilities. They have the potential to provide tested students with an unrecognized advantage over other students or an unrecognized disadvantage. In both of these situations, accurate interpretations cannot be made from the resulting scores. For example, English language learners might be provided with a simplified-language version of a test when in fact other test takers might also score higher if they were offered this accommodation. Research has shown that use of simplified language can, in fact, offer all students, not just those with a language deficit, an advantage on some tests (Abedi, Hofstetter et al., 2001; Abedi and Lord, 2001). This suggests that language simplification may have removed factors that were construct-irrelevant for all test-takers.

Alternatively, accommodations intended to compensate for deficits in English fluency may actually impede performance. For example, English language learners may actually be disadvantaged if they have not had experience with an accommodation they are offered, particularly if it is one that requires substantial time to use, such as offering the assessment in the native language when the language of instruction is English, or providing a glossary or bilingual dictionary. In these instances, test-takers' time and attention are diverted from the test itself and their scores may be depressed (Abedi, Lord, Hofstetter, and Baker, 2000).

Another challenge to administrators who need to assess English language learners is that, as noted above, while approximately 80 percent of the English language learners in U.S. schools are native Spanish speakers, the remaining 20 percent speak many different languages. States and districts with rapidly changing immigrant populations face the need to develop programs that are flexible enough to handle many different languages. They may lack the resources to easily assess the language skills of students from each linguistic background, and they may not be able to afford to offer accommodations that rely entirely or in part on the student's native language (e.g., offering a native-language version of the test, allowing students to respond in their native language, or offering a glossary or translated directions).

The principal accommodations offered to English language learners are shown in Table 2-4.

TABLE 2-4 Testing Accommodations for English Language Learners

Setting	Timing/Scheduling
• Small group • Individual administration • Separate location, study carrel • Preferential seating • Teacher facing student	• Extended testing time (same day) • Frequent, extra, longer breaks • Time of day most beneficial to student • Several (shorter) sessions • Testing over several days (some extended time) • Flexible scheduling (of subtests)

Presentation	Response
• Oral reading of questions in English • Explanation of directions • Translation of directions • Repetition of directions • Translation of test into native language • Person familiar with student administers test • Audio cassette • Clarification of words (spelling, defining, explaining) • Highlighting key words • Oral reading of directions • Use of an interpreter (sight translator) • Bilingual version of the test • Oral reading of questions in native language • Simplified/sheltered English version of test • Use of place markers to maintain place	• Student dictates answer, uses scribe • Student response in native language • Student marks answers in test booklet • Student types or uses machine

Other
• Use of bilingual word lists, dictionaries • Out-of-level testing • Use of brainstorming activities

SOURCE: Rivera et al. (2000, p. 34).

SUMMARY

This chapter has presented background information designed to illustrate several key points about the participation of students with disabilities and English language learners in large-scale assessments. First, students with disabilities and English language learners are an extremely diverse group. Including them in large-scale assessments so that their educational status and their needs will be addressed along with those of other students is not only important but a legal mandate for states. However, their diverse needs call for assessment approaches that are both flexible enough to evaluate what they know and can do and rigorous enough that the results can be safely compared with those from other assessments.

Second, the legal requirements and professional standards regarding the assessment of these two groups of students provide considerable guidance to those responsible for setting assessment policy and developing assessment tools. They have established both the necessity for testing students with disabilities and English language learners and the key questions of fairness that arise when they are tested. These sources, however, offer relatively little guidance with regard to the practical difficulties associated with testing these two groups. As a consequence, there is considerable variation around the country in the way these students are assessed.

Finally, a key tool used in assessing students in these two groups is accommodation. These measures, designed to overcome obstacles to testing that are irrelevant to the constructs being measured, have the potential to make it possible to obtain accurate results for students who could not be reliably assessed without them. Many different accommodations are in use around the country. The ways in which they are used, the variety in the ways they are applied, and the knowledge base about their effects on testing results are the focus of the remainder of the report.

3

Participation in NAEP and Other Large-Scale Assessments

A variety of factors can influence the rates at which students with disabilities and English language learners participate in large-scale assessments. Legislative mandates have established requirements that, in general, all such students should be included in statewide accountability programs, but these requirements do allow for the exclusion of a small number of students from assessments. These laws require that accommodations be provided for students who need them but offer relatively scant guidance for determining how and when the accommodations should be provided. The National Assessment of Educational Progress (NAEP) assessments have not been subject to the same legal requirements regarding participation, and until 1996 they did not permit accommodations. NAEP's participation rates for students with disabilities and English language learners have thus lagged behind those of state assessment programs. In this chapter, we present the information available on participation rates in NAEP and statewide assessments and discuss the implications of the available data.

PARTICIPATION RATES FOR NAEP

NAEP's Research Study on Providing Accommodations

In the early 1990s, students with individualized education programs (IEPs) could be excluded from NAEP if they were placed in general education classrooms (mainstreamed) less than 50 percent of the time or judged to be incapable of meaningful participation in the assessment. Some English language learners—defined as students whose native language was not English, who had been enrolled in an English speaking school for less than three years, or who were judged incapable of meaningful participation in the assessment—could also be excluded. Specifically, a NAEP publication describes the former procedures for these two groups in the following way (U.S. Department of Education National Center for Education Statistics, 1997).

> Prior to 1990, administrations of NAEP . . . relied on the judgment of school administrators as to whether or not the student could take the assessment. Beginning with the 1990 NAEP, schools were given guidelines informing them that they may exclude a student with a disability if the student is mainstreamed less than 50% of the time and is judged incapable of participating meaningfully in the assessment, OR, the IEP team or equivalent group determined that the student is incapable of participating meaningfully in the assessment. Schools were instructed to include students with disabilities if school staff believed the students were capable of taking the assessment. Schools were also instructed that when there was doubt, students should be included. (pp. 14-15)

> The NAEP procedures used prior to 1990 allowed schools to exclude sampled students if they were LEP and if local school personnel judged the students incapable of participating meaningfully in the assessment Beginning in 1990, NAEP instructions to schools for excluding LEP students from the assessment required the following conditions to be met: the student is a native speaker of a language other than English AND the student has been enrolled in an English-speaking school for less than 2 years (not including bilingual education programs) AND school officials judged the student to be incapable of taking the assessment. The guidelines also stated that when in doubt, the student was to be included in the assessment. (p. 41)

NAEP's sponsors took the first step in making the assessment more inclusive when they adopted a series of resolutions that established a plan for conducting research on the effects of including students with disabilities and English language learners in the assessment.

In these resolutions, NAEP's sponsors articulated the dual priorities of including students who can meaningfully take part in the assessment while maintaining the integrity of the trend data that are considered a key component of NAEP. The resolution and research plan provided what NAEP officials have described as both "a bridge to the future," because it would make NAEP more inclusive, and "a bridge to the past" (NRC, 2002a), because it would allow NAEP to continue to provide meaningful trend information. Protection of the capacity to report trend data was considered a necessary constraint on any changes in policies and procedures.

NAEP conducted a series of pilot studies in the early 1990s to examine the feasibility of allowing students to participate in the assessment with accommodations and then, in conjunction with the 1996 mathematics assessment, initiated a research plan. This plan called for data to be collected for three samples of tested students, referred to as S1, S2, and S3. For the S1 sample, administration procedures were handled in the same way as in the early 1990s, and students with special needs could be excluded from the assessment. For the S2 sample, revisions aimed at increasing participation were made to the criteria given to schools for determining whether to include students with special needs, but no accommodations or adaptations were offered. For state NAEP, the schools were split between S1 and S2. For national NAEP, a third sample of schools, S3, was identified, in which the revised inclusion criteria were used, and accommodations were permitted for students with disabilities and English language learners. These students were allowed to participate with the accommodations that they routinely received in their state or district testing.

Analyses of the 1996 data revealed no differences in inclusion rates between the S1 and S2 samples, so the S1 criteria were discontinued, and further research was based on samples of schools that applied either the revised criteria. Comparison of the S2 and S3 samples provided the opportunity to examine the net effects of both types of changes, both more lenient criteria for inclusion and the use of accommodations.

The research continued with the 1998 national and state NAEP reading assessment and the 2000 assessments (math and science at the national level in grades 4, 8, and 12 and at the state level in grades 4 and 8; reading at the national level in grade 4). Analyses of the 1998 and 2000 data revealed that providing accommodations did increase the number of students with disabilities and English language learners included in NAEP in grades 4 and 8.

Table 3-1 presents information from the research study on the participation rates of students with disabilities and English language learners in NAEP's reading and math assessments for fourth graders. Participation rates (column 6) were calculated by dividing the number of students assessed (column 5) by the number identified (column 4) and multiplying by 100. Thus, the table shows that the percentages of students with disabilities who participated in NAEP's fourth grade reading assessment were 13.8 percent in 1992 and 34.1 percent in 1994. These were years in which students with disabilities and English language learners could participate but no accommodations were allowed. Participation rates for the S2 (accommodations not allowed) and S3 (accommodations allowed) study samples are displayed separately for each of the years the study was in place.

Comparisons of the participation rates in a given year demonstrate the impact of providing accommodations. For example, for the 1998 fourth grade reading assessment, the participation rate for students with disabilities was 6.3 percentage points higher for the S3 sample than for the S2 sample. The median differences over assessment years between the participation rates when accommodations were not allowed and were allowed were 17.7 percent for students with disabilities and 21.3 percent for English language learners.

Table 3-2 presents this same information from the research study on the participation rates of students with disabilities and English language learners in NAEP's reading and math assessments for eighth graders. For eighth graders, the

TABLE 3-1 Results from NAEP's Research: Participation of Students with Disabilities (SWD) and English Language Learners (ELL) in Fourth Grade NAEP Reading and Math Assessments

(1)	(2)	(3)	(4) Students Identified		(5) Students Assessed		(6) Percent Participating	
Assessment	Year	Accommodation Permitted	SWD	ELL	SWD	ELL	SWD	ELL
Reading	1992	No	1,149	945	159	110	13.8	11.6
	1994	No	1,039	623	354	255	34.1	40.9
	1998—S2^a	No	490	527	243	204	49.6	38.7
	1998—S3^b	Yes	558	446	312	279	55.9	62.6
	Differences in participation rates for two 1998 samples						*6.3*	*23.9*
	2000—S2^a	No	524	356	229	215	43.7	60.4
	2000—S3^b	Yes	510	446	317	287	62.2	64.4
	Differences in participation rates for two 2000 samples						*18.5*	*4.0*
Math	1992	No	1,163	939	173	104	14.9	11.1
	1996—S2^a	No	359	142	206	75	57.4	52.8
	1996—S3^b	Yes	424	308	315	222	74.3	72.1
	Differences in participation rates for two 1996 samples						*16.9*	*19.3*
	2000—S2^a	No	672	454	292	265	43.5	58.4
	2000—S3^b	Yes	706	472	526	385	74.5	81.6
	Differences in participation rates for two 2000 samples						*31.0*	*23.2*

[a]Results from split sample study: Students taking this assessment were NOT allowed accommodations.
[b]Results from split sample study: Students taking this assessment WERE allowed accommodations.
SOURCE: Available: http://nces.ed.gov.

median differences over assessment years in the participation rates when accommodations were not allowed and were allowed were 21.0 percent for students with disabilities and 13.2 percent for English language learners.

NAEP's Reporting of Participation Rates

The committee examined reports from several administrations of NAEP to gather information on participation rates for the most recent assessment. Table 3-3 presents the national data for students with disabilities and English language learners for the 1998-2002 reading assessment. Table 3-4 shows results by state for students with disabilities for the grade 4 reading assessment in 1998 and 2002, and Table 3-5 shows these results for English language learners. We note that the method for displaying the results presented in these tables has been improved from previous years. In the past, participation rates at the national level were reported separately for students with disabilities and English language learners,

TABLE 3-2 Results from NAEP's Research: Participation of Students with
Disabilities (SWD) and English Language Learners (ELL) in Eighth Grade
NAEP Reading and Math Assessments

(1)	(2)	(3)	(4) Students Identified		(5) Students Assessed		(6) Percent Participating	
Assessment	Year	Accommodation Permitted	SWD	ELL	SWD	ELL	SWD	ELL
Reading	1992	No	1,522	836	199	86	13.1	10.3
	1994	No	1,323	444	344	121	26.0	27.3
	1998—S2[a]	No	975	449	451	315	46.3	70.2
	1998—S3[b]	Yes	865	447	582	338	67.3	75.6
	Differences in participation rates for two 1998 samples						*21.0*	*5.4*
Math	1992	No	1,538	838	215	88	14.0	10.5
	1996[a]	No	310	106	161	68	51.9	64.2
	1996[b]	Yes	557	226	374	175	67.1	77.4
	Differences in participation rates for two 1996 samples						*15.2*	*13.2*
	2000[a]	No	1,316	551	597	341	45.4	61.9
	2000[b]	Yes	1,206	471	804	368	66.7	78.1
	Differences in participation rates for two 2000 samples						*21.3*	*16.2*

[a]Results from split sample study: Students taking this assessment were NOT allowed accommodations.
[b]Results from split sample study: Students taking this assessment WERE allowed accommodations.
SOURCE: Available: http://nces.ed.gov.

but NAEP state-level reports combined participation data for the two groups. An
example of the way these data were previously presented is shown in Table 3-6.
With the state-level data for these two groups combined, it was impossible either
to track participation rates separately for the two groups or to make comparisons
between participation rates in state assessments and in NAEP (incomplete data
from state assessments have also been an impediment to making these comparisons; that issue is discussed below).

The committee had intended to make a recommendation about the reporting
of state-level participation rates, but before our deliberations were completed,
NAEP for the first time presented the participation rates for students with disabilities and English language learners separately in both state and national
reports. In the committee's judgment, the revised version of the NAEP tables is a
significant improvement and we encourage NAEP's sponsors to continue to
provide these data.

TABLE 3-3 Students with Disabilities (SWD) and/or Limited English Proficient (LEP) Students Identified, Excluded, and Assessed, When Accommodations Were Permitted, Grades 4, 8, and 12 Public and Nonpublic Schools: 1998–2002 for Reading

	1998		2000		2002	
	Number of Students	Weighted Percentage of Students Sampled	Number of Students	Weighted Percentage of Students Sampled	Number of Students	Weighted Percentage of Students Sampled
Grade 4						
SD and/or LEP students						
Identified	973	16	906	18	28,073	19
Excluded	393	6	316	6	10,307	6
Assessed	580	10	590	12	17,766	13
Without accommodations	413	7	476	10	11,913	9
With accommodations	167	3	114	2	5,853	4
SD students						
Identified	558	10	510	11	19,936	12
Excluded	246	4	193	4	8,042	5
Assessed	312	6	317	7	11,894	7
Without accommodations	179	3	209	5	6,631	4
With accommodations	133	3	108	2	5,263	3
LEP students						
Identified	446	6	446	8	10,334	8
Excluded	167	2	159	3	3,410	2
Assessed	279	4	287	5	6,924	6
Without accommodations	238	3	273	5	6,020	6
With accommodations	41	1	14	#	904	1

continued

Grade 8

SD and/or LEP students					
Identified	20,137	17	—	—	1,252	12
Excluded	7,135	5	—	—	368	4
Assessed	13,002	11	—	—	884	9
Without accommodations	8,598	8	—	—	678	6
With accommodations	4,404	4	—	—	206	2
SD students					
Identified	16,159	12	—	—	865	10
Excluded	5,939	4	—	—	283	3
Assessed	10,220	8	—	—	582	7
Without accommodations	6,074	5	—	—	404	5
With accommodations	4,146	3	—	—	178	2
LEP students					
Identified	5,516	6	—	—	447	3
Excluded	1,907	2	—	—	109	1
Assessed	3,609	4	—	—	338	2
Without accommodations	3,113	4	—	—	307	2
With accommodations	496	#	—	—	31	#

Grade 12

SD and/or LEP students					
Identified	1,556	12	—	—	975	7
Excluded	616	4	—	—	327	2
Assessed	940	8	—	—	648	5
Without accommodations	673	6	—	—	532	4
With accommodations	267	2	—	—	116	1
SD students					
Identified	1,231	9	—	—	649	6
Excluded	535	3	—	—	285	2
Assessed	696	6	—	—	364	4
Without accommodations	446	4	—	—	266	3
With accommodations	250	2	—	—	98	1

TABLE 3-3 Continued

	1998		2000		2002	
	Number of Students	Weighted Percentage of Students Sampled	Number of Students	Weighted Percentage of Students Sampled	Number of Students	Weighted Percentage of Students Sampled
LEP students						
Identified	353	2	—	—	419	3
Excluded	58	#	—	—	125	1
Assessed	295	2	—	—	294	3
Without accommodations	277	2	—	—	266	2
With accommodations	18	#	—	—	28	#

— Data were not collected at grades 8 and 12 in 2000.

Percentage rounds to zero.

NOTE: Within each grade level, the combined SD/LEP portion of the table is not a sum of the separate SD and LEP portions because some students were identified as both SD and LEP. Such students would be counted separately in the bottom portions but counted only once in the top portion. Within each portion of the table, percentages may not add to totals, due to rounding.

The number of students at grades 4 and 8 are larger in 2002 than in previous years because the 2002 national sample was based on the combined sample of students in each participating state, plus an additional sample from nonparticipating states as well as a sample from private schools.

SOURCE: From U.S. Department of Education, Institute of Education Sciences, National Center for Education Statistics, National Assessment of Educational Progress, 1998, 2000, and 2002 Reading Assessments.

TABLE 3-4 Percentage of Students with Disabilities (SD) Identified, Excluded, and Assessed, When Accommodations Were Permitted, Grade 4 Public Schools: By State, 1998 and 2002 for Reading

	1998 SD Students					2002 SD Students				
	Identified	Excluded	Assessed	Assessed without Accommodations	Assessed with Accommodations	Identified	Excluded	Assessed	Assessed without Accommodations	Assessed with Accommodations
Nation (Public)	12	5	7	4	3	13	5	8	4	4
Alabama	13	8	4	3	1	13	2	11	8	2
Arizona	10	5	5	4	1	11	5	7	5	2
Arkansas	10	4	6	4	2	12	4	7	5	2
California‡	6	3	2	2	1	7	3	4	3	1
Connecticut	14	7	7	4	3	13	4	9	4	6
Delaware	14	1	12	9	4	15	7	8	3	5
Florida	14	5	9	5	4	17	5	13	6	7
Georgia	9	4	6	3	3	10	3	7	4	3
Hawaii	10	4	7	5	1	12	4	8	3	4
Idaho	—	—	—	—	—	13	4	9	7	2
Illinois‡	10	3	6	4	2	13	4	9	4	5
Indiana	—	—	—	—	—	12	4	8	6	2
Iowa‡	14	5	9	6	3	15	7	8	3	5
Kansas‡	9	3	6	3	3	14	4	10	4	5
Kentucky	12	7	5	3	2	11	8	4	2	1
Louisiana	14	7	7	2	5	19	10	8	3	5
Maine	15	7	7	4	3	16	6	10	5	6
Maryland	11	5	6	2	4	12	6	6	4	2
Massachusetts	16	4	12	7	5	16	4	12	3	9

continued

TABLE 3-4 Continued

	1998 SD Students					2002 SD Students				
	Identified	Excluded	Assessed	Assessed without Accommodations	Assessed with Accommodations	Identified	Excluded	Assessed	Assessed without Accommodations	Assessed with Accommodations
Michigan	9	5	3	2	1	11	7	4	3	1
Minnesota‡	12	3	9	6	3	13	4	10	6	3
Mississippi	7	4	3	2	#	7	4	3	2	1
Missouri	14	6	7	3	4	15	8	7	4	3
Montana‡	10	2	7	5	2	13	5	8	4	4
Nebraska	—	—	—	—	—	18	4	13	7	6
Nevada	10	6	4	4	1	12	5	7	5	2
New Mexico	14	7	7	5	2	15	7	9	6	3
New York‡	9	4	5	1	4	14	6	8	2	5
North Carolina	14	6	8	2	6	17	10	6	3	4
North Dakota‡	—	—	—	—	—	16	5	11	8	3
Ohio	—	—	—	—	—	13	8	5	3	2
Oklahoma	13	9	5	3	1	17	5	13	8	5
Oregon	14	4	10	6	4	16	5	10	7	3
Pennsylvania	—	—	—	—	—	13	4	9	4	5
Rhode Island	14	5	10	6	3	19	3	15	6	10
South Carolina	15	7	8	5	3	16	4	11	8	3
Tennessee‡	12	3	9	7	2	11	3	8	6	1
Texas	14	7	8	5	2	14	8	6	5	2
Utah	10	4	6	4	1	12	4	6	5	3
Vermont	—	—	—	—	—	13	5	9	3	6
Virginia	14	6	8	4	4	14	8	6	3	3

Washington‡	11	4	8	5	3	13	4	9	6	4
West Virginia	12	8	4	2	1	15	10	5	3	2
Wisconsin‡	13	7	6	4	2	13	6	8	3	4
Wyoming	13	3	10	6	4	14	2	12	5	7
Other Jurisdictions										
District of Columbia	10	6	4	2	2	14	7	7	3	4
DDESS[1]	7	3	4	2	2	10	3	7	3	4
DoDDS[2]	6	2	4	3	1	9	2	7	4	3
Guam	—	—	—	—	0	7	4	3	2	1
Virgin Islands	4	3	1	1	0	3	1	2	2	#

— Indicates that the jurisdiction did not participate.

Percentage rounds to zero.

‡ Indicates that the jurisdiction did not meet one or more of the guidelines for school participation in 2002.

[1] Department of Defense Domestic Dependent Elementary and Secondary Schools.

[2] Department of Defense Dependents Schools (Overseas).

NOTE: Percentages may not add to totals, due to rounding.

SOURCE: From U.S. Department of Education, Institute of Education Sciences, National Center for Education Statistics, National Assessment of Educational Progress, 1998 and 2002 Reading Assessments.

TABLE 3-5 Percentage of Limited English Proficient (LEP) Students Identified, Excluded, and Assessed, When Accommodations Were Permitted, Grade 4 Public Schools: By State, 1998 and 2002 for Reading

	1998 LEP Students					2002 LEP Students				
	Identified	Excluded	Assessed	Assessed without Accommodations	Assessed with Accommodations	Identified	Excluded	Assessed	Assessed without Accommodations	Assessed with Accommodations
Nation (Public)	5	2	3	3	1	9	2	7	6	1
Alabama	#	#	#	0	#	1	#	1	1	#
Arizona	14	6	7	6	1	21	5	16	15	1
Arkansas	1	1	1	1	0	3	1	3	3	#
California‡	26	12	14	13	1	29	3	26	26	#
Connecticut	5	4	1	1	#	4	2	2	2	#
Delaware	3	#	2	2	#	3	2	1	1	#
Florida	5	1	3	3	#	10	3	7	5	2
Georgia	2	1	#	#	#	4	1	2	2	#
Hawaii	6	2	4	4	0	8	2	6	4	1
Idaho	—	—	—	—	—	7	1	6	5	#
Illinois‡	5	3	2	2	#	9	4	5	4	1
Indiana	—	—	—	—	—	2	1	1	1	0
Iowa‡	1	1	1	1	0	2	1	1	1	#
Kansas‡	3	1	2	2	#	7	2	6	4	2
Kentucky	1	#	#	#	#	1	#	#	#	#
Louisiana	1	1	1	1	0	1	1	1	#	#
Maine	#	0	#	#	#	1	#	#	#	#
Maryland	2	1	2	1	#	3	2	1	1	#
Massachusetts	4	2	2	2	1	4	2	2	1	1
Michigan	2	1	1	1	#	3	1	2	2	#

State										
Minnesota‡	4	1	3	3	1	7	2	5	4	1
Mississippi	#	0	#	#	0	#	#	#	#	0
Missouri	1	#	#	#	#	2	1	1	1	#
Montana‡	#	0	#	0	#	2	1	1	1	#
Nebraska	—	—	—	—	—	4	2	3	2	#
Nevada	10	6	4	4	#	18	7	11	10	1
New Mexico	16	4	12	11	1	27	6	21	19	2
New York‡	5	4	1	1	0	6	3	3	1	1
North Carolina	2	1	1	1	#	5	3	1	1	1
North Dakota‡	—	—	—	—	—	2	1	2	1	#
Ohio	—	—	—	—	—	1	1	1	1	0
Oklahoma	2	#	1	1	0	5	1	4	3	1
Oregon	7	2	5	4	1	12	4	8	6	2
Pennsylvania	—	—	—	—	—	2	1	1	1	#
Rhode Island	6	3	4	3	1	9	3	5	4	2
South Carolina	1	#	1	1	0	2	1	1	1	#
Tennessee‡	1	1	#	#	0	3	1	3	3	#
Texas	13	7	6	6	#	16	5	11	10	1
Utah	5	2	3	2	#	9	3	7	5	1
Vermont	—	—	—	—	—	2	#	1	1	#
Virginia	2	1	1	1	1	6	3	3	2	1
Washington‡	4	2	3	2	#	3	1	2	2	1
West Virginia	#	#	#	#	0	#	#	#	#	#
Wisconsin‡	3	1	2	1	#	6	3	3	2	0
Wyoming	1	1	#	#	#	5	1	4	3	1

continued

TABLE 3-5 Continued

	1998 LEP Students					2002 LEP Students				
	Identified	Excluded	Assessed	Assessed without Accommodations	Assessed with Accommodations	Identified	Excluded	Assessed	Assessed without Accommodations	Assessed with Accommodations
Other Jurisdictions										
District of Columbia	7	3	4	2	1	7	3	4	3	2
DDESS[1]	1	1	#	0	#	6	2	4	3	1
DoDDS[2]	2	1	1	1	#	8	1	7	6	1
Guam	—	—	—	—	—	36	5	31	25	6
Virgin Islands	4	2	2	1	1	5	2	3	3	1

— Indicates that the jurisdiction did not participate.

Percentage rounds to zero.

‡ Indicates that the jurisdiction did not meet one or more of the guidelines for school participation in 2002.

[1] Department of Defense Domestic Dependent Elementary and Secondary Schools.

[2] Department of Defense Dependents Schools (Overseas).

NOTE: Percentages may not add to totals, due to rounding.

SOURCE: From U.S. Department of Education, Institute of Education Sciences, National Center for Education Statistics, National Assessment of Educational Progress, 1998 and 2002 Reading Assessments.

PARTICIPATION RATES FOR STATE ASSESSMENTS

The committee attempted to obtain information on the participation rates of the two student groups in statewide assessment programs in order to make comparisons with NAEP's participation rates. However, we discovered that this information is not readily available. The most comprehensive source of data on state assessments is maintained by the Council of Chief State School Officers through their annual survey of state student assessment programs (Council of Chief State School Officers, 2002). With this survey, the council collects information about exemptions from statewide assessments; that is, the survey asks states if the number of special education or limited English proficient exemptions increased, decreased, or stayed the same over the past two to three years. However, the survey report does not provide data that could be used to calculate participation rates.

Two additional sources were identified. Some information on participation rates for students with disabilities in state assessments is available from the National Center on Education Outcomes. Based on their review of states' biennial performance reports to the U.S. Department of Education, Thurlow et al. (2002) were able to obtain enough information for each state to calculate participation rates for all of the states. However, data were not provided for all of the tests states administer or in all of the grades assessed. Thus, it was not possible to examine these participation rates by grade level or by the subject matter of the test. Thurlow et al. reported a participation rate for every state, but in some states it is the only rate that could be calculated, while in others it is the highest of the rates calculated.

In the Thurlow report, state participation rates were calculated as follows: the numerator was the number of students with disabilities participating in the assessment; the denominator was the number of participating students with disabilities, plus the number taking the alternate assessment, plus the number not tested, which should equal the total number of students with disabilities enrolled in special education services in the state. Based on these calculations, the participation rates for students with disabilities were 90 percent or higher in 19 states, between 75 and 89 percent in 17 states, between 50 and 74 percent in 5 states, and between 25 and 49 percent in 1 state.

According to the authors of that report, the required analyses were quite complex, and determining the denominator for the participation rate was challenging. This was the first time analyses like this had been undertaken, primarily because in the past the Department of Education requirement to report results using a standard structure was not in place (M. Thurlow, personal communication, December 16, 2003).

In addition, *Education Week* (Education Week, 2004) recently reported the results of a survey of the states and the District of Columbia designed to gather data on the inclusion of students with disabilities in state testing and accountability

TABLE 3-6 Percentage of Students with Disabilities (SD) and/or Limited English Proficient (LEP) Students Identified, Excluded, and Assessed, When Accommodations Were Permitted, Grade 4 Public Schools: By State, 1998 and 2002 for Reading

| | 1998 SD and/or LEP Students | | | | | All Students |
	Identified	Excluded	Assessed	Assessed without Accommodations	Assessed with Accommodations	Assessed without Accommodations
Nation (Public)	18	7	11	7	3	90
Alabama	13	8	4	3	1	90
Arizona	22	10	12	10	1	88
Arkansas	11	5	6	4	2	93
California‡	31	14	16	15	1	84
Connecticut	18	10	8	5	3	87
Delaware	16	1	15	11	4	95
Florida	18	6	12	8	5	89
Georgia	11	5	6	3	3	93
Hawaii	15	5	10	9	1	94
Idaho	—	—	—	—	—	—
Illinois‡	14	6	8	6	2	92
Indiana	—	—	—	—	—	—
Iowa‡	15	5	10	7	3	92
Kansas‡	12	4	8	5	4	93
Kentucky	13	7	5	3	2	90
Louisiana	15	7	8	3	5	88
Maine	15	7	7	4	3	90
Maryland	13	6	8	4	4	90
Massachusetts	19	5	14	9	5	90
Michigan	10	6	4	3	1	93
Minnesota‡	15	3	12	9	3	94
Mississippi	7	4	3	2	#	95
Missouri	14	6	8	3	4	89
Montana‡	10	2	7	5	2	96
Nebraska	—	—	—	—	—	—
Nevada	20	11	9	8	1	88
New Mexico	28	9	18	16	2	88
New York‡	14	7	7	2	4	88
North Carolina	15	7	9	3	6	88
North Dakota‡	—	—	—	—	—	—
Ohio	—	—	—	—	—	—
Oklahoma	15	9	6	5	1	90
Oregon	20	6	14	10	4	90
Pennsylvania	—	—	—	—	—	—
Rhode Island	20	7	13	9	4	89
South Carolina	16	8	9	6	3	90

2002
SD and/or LEP Students

Identified	Excluded	Assessed	Assessed without Accom- modations	Assessed with Accom- modations	All Students Assessed without Accom- modations
21	7	14	10	4	89
14	3	12	9	2	95
28	8	21	18	3	90
14	5	10	8	2	93
34	5	29	28	1	94
16	5	11	5	6	89
17	8	9	4	5	87
25	7	18	10	8	85
13	4	9	6	3	93
18	6	12	7	5	89
17	4	13	11	2	93
20	7	14	8	6	87
13	5	9	7	2	93
16	8	8	3	5	87
19	5	14	7	7	88
12	8	4	3	1	91
19	10	9	3	6	84
17	6	11	5	6	88
14	7	7	5	2	92
19	6	13	4	9	85
14	7	6	5	1	92
19	5	13	10	4	91
7	4	3	2	1	95
16	9	8	4	3	88
15	6	8	4	4	89
21	5	15	9	6	88
27	10	17	14	3	87
37	10	27	23	4	85
18	8	9	3	6	86
19	12	7	3	4	84
18	5	13	9	3	91
14	8	5	4	2	90
21	5	15	10	5	89
25	8	17	13	4	88
14	5	10	4	5	90
25	6	19	8	11	84
16	5	12	9	3	92

continued

TABLE 3-6 Continued

1998
SD and/or LEP Students

	Identified	Excluded	Assessed	Assessed without Accommodations	Assessed with Accommodations	All Students Assessed without Accommodations
Tennessee[‡]	13	4	9	8	2	95
Texas	26	13	14	11	3	85
Utah	14	6	8	6	2	92
Vermont	—	—	—	—	—	—
Virginia	15	6	9	4	5	89
Washington[‡]	15	5	10	7	3	92
West Virginia	12	8	4	2	1	90
Wisconsin[‡]	16	8	8	5	3	89
Wyoming	14	3	10	6	4	93
Other Jurisdictions						
District of Columbia	16	9	8	5	3	89
DDESS[1]	8	4	4	2	2	94
DoDDS[2]	7	3	4	3	1	96
Guam	—	—	—	—	—	—
Virgin Islands	8	5	3	2	1	94

— Indicates that the jurisdiction did not participate.

Percentage rounds to zero.

‡ Indicates that the jurisdiction did not meet one or more of the guidelines for school participation in 2002.

[1] Department of Defense Domestic Dependent Elementary and Secondary Schools.

[2] Department of Defense Dependents Schools (Overseas).

systems. Their publication, *Quality Counts 2004,* reports participation rates in state assessments in fourth, eighth, and tenth grade reading and mathematics assessments. Participation rates were calculated by dividing the number of students with disabilities who took the test in each grade level and subject area by the number of students with disabilities enrolled in each grade level and subject area. Table 3-7 summarizes their findings.

The authors note that 10 states and the District of Columbia were unable to provide the requested data for the 2002-2003 school year. In some states, this was because the data had not yet been reviewed and confirmed. In other cases the data could not be reported according to the specified grade levels. Some states could only compare the test-taking rates of special education students with those for all students (including those with disabilities), not just general education students,

2002
SD and/or LEP Students

Identified	Excluded	Assessed	Assessed without Accommodations	Assessed with Accommodations	All Students Assessed without Accommodations
14	3	10	9	1	95
27	11	16	14	2	87
19	6	13	9	4	91
15	5	10	4	6	89
18	10	8	5	3	87
15	5	11	7	4	92
16	10	5	3	2	87
19	8	10	5	5	87
17	3	15	7	7	90
19	8	11	5	5	86
14	4	10	6	4	92
16	3	13	9	4	93
39	7	32	26	6	87
7	3	4	4	1	97

NOTE: Percentages may not add to totals, due to rounding.
SOURCE: U.S. Department of Education, Institute of Education Sciences, National Center for Education Statistics, National Assessment of Educational Progress, 1998 and 2002 Reading Assessments.

TABLE 3-7 Participation Rates for Students with Disabilities in State Assessments for the 2002-2003 School Year

Participation Rate Range (%)	Fourth Grade Reading	Fourth Grade Math	Eighth Grade Reading	Eighth Grade Math	Tenth Grade Reading	Tenth Grade Math
95-100	29[a]	31	21	22	15	15
90-94	5	2	11	10	8	6
85-89	3	4	5	4	7	7
40-84	3	3	4	4	8	9

[a]Number of states with participation rate in the specified range.
SOURCE: *Education Week* (2004, pp. 84-85).

and some states had "coding problems" (*Quality Counts*, p. 76). Like Thurlow, the authors note that compilation of these data was not straightforward, and they note that "differences in participation rates across states reflect, in part, the fact that states do not count students the same way when calculating such data" (p. 76). They cite the following as sources of differences:

- If states did not have tests in place in the targeted grades, participation rates were based on tests for the next closest grade level.
- If states did not have results for the 2002-2003 school year, participation rates were based on the most recent results available.
- While all states count students with disabilities who take state tests without accommodations or with "standard" accommodations in their participation rates, only 26 states and the District of Columbia count those who take state tests with modifications.[1]
- Fourteen of the states include students who took out-of-level tests in their participation rates.
- While most states counted students who took alternate assessments in their participation rates, California and Indiana excluded them from their participation rates.

The participation rate data reported above all pertain to students with disabilities. We were unable to obtain data that would permit calculations of participation rates for English language learners.

SUMMARY

The provision of accommodations has clearly increased the overall participation of students with special needs in NAEP, but significant variations in accommodation policies, both among the states and between states and NAEP, remain an important issue to consider in evaluating the comparability of data about students with disabilities and English language learners. Nevertheless, state assessment programs vary in the constructs they are measuring, both from one another and from NAEP, and these differences account for some of the variation in policies. To the extent that the rates are significantly different, inferences made from comparisons of results from NAEP and state-level assessments for these two groups must be limited. While other differences between NAEP and state-level assessments limit the kinds of inferences that can be made from comparisons in any case (National Research Council, 1999b), it is nevertheless true that gross differences in performance on NAEP and a state assessment are often cited as reasons to further explore the state assessment results and possible reasons for the

---

[1]"Modifications" is used here as a synonym, for "accommodations."

discrepancy. It has been proposed that NAEP results could serve as an informal check on the results obtained through the assessments required under the No Child Left Behind Act (National Assessment Governing Board, 2002a). However, for even an informal comparison to be useful as an indication that NAEP and a statewide assessment are yielding results that do not contradict one another, the participation rates for the two groups on each assessment must also be compared.

There may be some legitimate reasons why the rates at which students with disabilities and English language learners participate in NAEP may never equal the participation rates for states. Both NAEP's purpose and the specific constructs it measures are undoubtedly different in some ways from those of state assessments. NAEP is a low-stakes assessment to which tested students and their teachers attach relatively little importance because of its lack of immediate consequences for them. NAEP assessments are based on a sampling procedure (discussed in greater detail in Chapter 4), rather than the premise that it will provide individual results for every student. Moreover, some states offer alternate assessment options for some students with disabilities and English language learners that cannot be offered by NAEP. Nevertheless, important policy decisions made at the federal, state, and local levels are influenced by NAEP results. These decisions will affect all the students in the relevant jurisdiction and therefore should be based on complete information about all of the students in that jurisdiction. NAEP is designed to report results for the nation as a whole, and therefore it is the committee's view that it should be guided by the same goal of maximizing participation rates that has been imposed on the states through legislation, so that information about all students can be obtained.

Currently, one reason that students with disabilities and English language learners are not able to participate in NAEP may be that the accommodations they need are not provided or not allowed by NAEP. It may be informative for NAEP to collect information on the extent to which students with disabilities and English language learners are not able to participate as a consequence of NAEP's policies regarding accommodations, and specifically about the types of accommodations students require that NAEP does not allow or provide. This effort could lead to increased participation rates on NAEP, as well as to a better representation of the academic achievement of the nation's student population.

Based on the information we have reviewed, the committee concludes that:

CONCLUSION 3-1: The increased use of accommodations with NAEP assessments has corresponded to increased participation rates for students with disabilities and English language learners.

4

Factors That Affect the Accuracy of NAEP's Estimates of Achievement

The purpose of the National Assessment of Educational Progress (NAEP) is to provide reports to the nation on the academic achievement of all students in grades 4, 8, and 12. NAEP accomplishes this through sampling, a process similar to those used in political polling, marketing surveys, and other contexts, in which only a scientifically selected portion of the target population, the group about whom data are needed, is actually assessed. This process is complex, and ensuring that it is conducted correctly is critical to the integrity of NAEP's reported results.

There are a number of factors that make the sampling process a challenge for the NAEP officials who are responsible for it, and that make interpreting the results difficult for users of the data who want to understand the academic achievement of students in the United States. For one, the sampling process is affected by decisions made at the local level about which of the sampled students who have a disability or are English language learners should participate in NAEP. The process is also dependent on the consistency with which a variety of procedures that are part of the administration of NAEP assessments are applied in local settings around the country. This chapter provides a description of the way NAEP sampling works and discussion of several factors that complicate it. We explore the variability in state policies for identifying students with disabilities and English language learners and the variability in state policies regarding allowable accommodations on state assessments, and we consider ways in which local decision making affects the integrity of NAEP samples and its results.

NAEP SAMPLING PROCEDURES

Because NAEP is designed to provide estimates of the performance of large groups of students in more than five separate subject areas and at three different stages of schooling, it would not be practical to test all of the students about whom data are sought in all subjects. Not only would each student be subjected to a prohibitively large amount of testing time in order to cover all of the targeted subject matter, but schools would also be unacceptably disrupted by such a burden. The solution is to assess only a fraction of the nation's students, evaluating each participating student on only a portion of the targeted subject matter. In order to be sure all of the material in each subject area is covered, developers design the assessment in blocks, each representing only a portion of the material specified in the NAEP framework for that subject. These blocks are administered according to a matrix sampling procedure, through which each student takes only two or three blocks in a variety of combinations. Statistical procedures are then used to link these results and project the performance to the broader population of the nation's students (U.S. Department of Education, National Center for Education Statistics, and Office of Educational Research and Improvement, 2001).

NAEP's estimates of proficiency are based on scientific samples of the population of interest, such as fourth grade students nationwide. In other words, the percentage of students in the total group of fourth graders who fall into each of the categories about which data are sought—such as girls, boys, members of various ethnic groups, and residents of urban, rural, or suburban areas—is calculated. A sample—a much smaller number of children—can then be identified whose proportions approximate those of the target population. Data are collected about other kinds of characteristics as well, including such information as parents' education levels, the type of school in which students are enrolled (public/private, large/small), and whether students have disabilities or are English language learners. In this way, NAEP reports can provide answers to a wide variety of questions about the percentages of students in each of a variety of groups, the relative performance of different groups, and the relationships among achievement and a wide variety of academic and background characteristics.

The sampling for NAEP is based on data received from schools about their students' characteristics as well as other factors. The selection of students in each school identified for NAEP participation is crucial to the representativeness of the overall sampling and the resulting estimates of performance. Local administrators are given lists of students who are to participate and instructions as to what adjustments to this list are permitted in response to absences and other factors that may affect participation. However, in the case of both students with disabilities and English language learners, which students ultimately remain in the sample depends in part on decisions made at the local level. These decisions are discussed in greater detail below.

COMPARABILITY OF NAEP SAMPLES ACROSS STATES

As was mentioned in Chapter 1, decision making about the identification of students with disabilities and English language learners, their inclusion in large-scale assessments, and the testing accommodations they need is guided by federal legislation (although far more detailed guidance is provided regarding students with disabilities than English language learners). It is up to states, however, to develop policies for complying with legislative requirements, and consequently the policies and the way they are interpreted vary from state to state, in some cases considerably. The variation in state policies has particular implications for NAEP. Decisions made at the state and local level affect NAEP's results and the ways in which they can be interpreted.

For each administration NAEP officials identify a sample of students to participate in the assessment, and they provide guidelines for administering it. However, school-level officials influence the process in several ways. First, as they are developing the sample, NAEP officials make no attempt to identify students with disabilities or English language learners themselves; rather, the percentages of those students who end up in the sample reflect decisions that have already been made at the school level; these decisions are guided by state policies, which vary. Second, NAEP officials leave it to school-level staff, who are knowledgeable about students' educational functioning levels, to determine whether selected students who have a disability or are English language learners can meaningfully participate. In general, this process is guided by the policy set forth in the NAEP 2003 Assessment Administrators' Manual (U.S. Department of Education, National Center for Education Statistics, and Office of Educational Research and Improvement, 2003, pp. 4-19). Finally, NAEP officials provide lists of allowable accommodations for each of its assessments, but here as well it is school-level staff who decide which accommodations are appropriate for their students and which of those allowed in NAEP they are in a position to offer. Thus, differences in policies and procedures both among and within states can affect who participates in NAEP and the way in which students participate.

According to the most recent legislation, the purpose of NAEP is "to provide, in a timely manner, a fair and accurate measurement of student academic achievement and reporting of trends in such achievement in reading, mathematics, and other subject matter as specified in this section" (Section 303 of HR 3801). The legislation further indicates that the commissioner for education statistics shall:

> (a) use a random sampling process which is consistent with relevant, widely accepted professional assessment standards and that produces data that are representative on a national and regional basis;
>
> (b) conduct a national assessment and collect and report assessment data, including achievement data trends, in a valid and reliable manner on student academic achievement in public and private elementary schools and secondary schools at least once every two years, in grades 4 and 8 in reading and mathematics;

(c) conduct a national assessment and collect and report assessment data, including achievement data trends, in a valid and reliable manner on student academic achievement [in] public and private schools in reading and mathematics in grade 12 in regularly scheduled intervals, but at least as often as such assessments were conducted prior to the date of enactment of the No Child Left Behind Act of 2001.

Both intrastate and interstate variability in the policies and procedures that determine which students participate and which accommodations they receive have implications for the interpretation of NAEP results. First, local decision making will affect the composition of a state sample, and thus the characteristics of the sample may vary across states in unintended and perhaps unrecognized ways. Likewise, local decisions about which accommodations a student requires will affect the conditions under which scores are obtained. This means that a state's results are subject to these locally made decisions, which may be based on criteria that vary from school to school in a state. Moreover, national NAEP results, in which scores are aggregated across states, are also subject to these locally made decisions. Finally, a key objective for NAEP is to characterize the achievement of the school-age population in the United States, yet the extent to which NAEP results are representative of the entire population depends on the locally made decisions that affect the samples.

Identifying and Classifying Students with Disabilities and English Language Learners

Determining which students should be classified as disabled in some way or as an English language learner is thus critical to ensuring that these groups of students are adequately represented, but making these classifications is far more complicated than many people recognize. In both cases, the specific situations that may call for such a classification vary widely, and there is no universally used or accepted method to use in making these judgments, particularly for English language learners. In general, decisions about whether and how specific students should be tested in NAEP are derived from previous decisions about those students' educational needs and placement, so it is important to understand how these decisions are made.

Identifying Students with Disabilities[1]

The process of identifying and classifying students with disabilities and determining their eligibility for special education typically involves three steps:

---

[1]Text in this section has been adapted from the reports of the National Research Council's Committee on Goals 2000 and the Inclusion of Students with Disabilities (National Research Council, 1997a) and the Committee on Minority Representation in Special Education (National Research Council, 2002a).

referral, which generally begins with the teacher; evaluation; and placement. Once an individual is identified as having a disability, a determination is made as to whether he or she qualifies for special education and related services. Under the Individuals with Disabilities Education Act (IDEA), eligibility for special education services is based on two criteria: first, the individual must meet the criteria for at least one of the 13 disabilities recognized in the IDEA (or the counterpart categories in state law) and, second, the individual must require special education or related services in order to receive an appropriate education. If both the disability diagnosis and special education need are confirmed, then the student has the right to an individualized education program (IEP). The IEP will also specify accommodations required for instructional purposes and for testing.

Although the IDEA is explicit about the procedures for identifying students as having a disability, significant variability exists in the way procedures are implemented. For some kinds of disabilities (such as physical or sensory ones), the criteria are clear. However, for others, such as learning disabilities, mild mental retardation, and serious emotional disturbance, the criteria are much less clear and the implementation practices are more variable.

States and districts do not have to adopt the disability categories in the federal laws and regulations (Hehir, 1996), and classification practices vary significantly from place to place; variation exists, for example, in the names given to categories, key dimensions on which the diagnosis is made, and criteria for determining eligibility (National Research Council, 1997a). This variability led the Committee on Goals 2000 and the Inclusion of Students with Disabilities to note that "it is entirely possible for students with identical characteristics to be diagnosed as having a disability in one state but not in another, or to have the categorical designation change with a move across states lines" (National Research Council, 1997a, p. 75).

Another source of variability is the referral process. Many of the referrals are made by classroom teachers. However, local norms are applied in making the judgment that achievement is acceptable or unacceptable. That is, whether a teacher perceives a student's level of achievement as acceptable or unacceptable varies as a function of the typical or average level of achievement in that student's classroom. It is the classroom teacher who compares the student with others and decides whether referral is appropriate (National Research Council, 2002a, p. 227). Special education referral rates can also be affected by policies and practices in a school system. The availability of other special programs, such as remedial reading and Title I services, can affect the number of students referred for special education (National Research Council, 1997a, p. 71).

Educators also face competing incentives in serving students who may have disabilities. For example, financial pressures on school districts and a lack of adequate federal and state support may make local officials reluctant to refer students for special education services even when they seem to meet relevant eligibility criteria (National Research Council, 1997a, p. 55). At the same time, staff in some schools may view their special education program as a kind of organizational safety valve that allows teachers to remove disruptive students from their classrooms, or that provides an alternative for vocal parents wanting additional assistance for their children (National Research Council, 1997a, p. 54). Consequently, schools may refer students for special education services when other remedies are more appropriate. Although none of these reasons is an adequate or even legitimate basis for deciding whether students are eligible for services, they represent the realities of local implementation. Educators' efforts to balance their responsibilities to serve all students, interpret applicable legal requirements for individual children, work within existing fiscal and organizational constraints, and respond to parental concerns may yield discrepancies, with the result that similar students might receive services in one school and be ineligible for them in another (National Research Council, 1997a, p. 55).

The requirement that the IEP be tailored to individual students' needs has also led to variability in the implementation of the IDEA. Evaluation, placement, and programming decisions for students with disabilities are intended to be idiosyncratic and to focus on the specific needs of the individual. The IEP process is designed this way so that the tendency for institutions to standardize their procedures will be countered by pressure from parents and special education staff to provide each student with the education and services he or she needs (National Research Council, 1997a). Because the IEP is the paramount determinant of matters affecting the education of students with disabilities, including participation in assessment and accommodations, this is a critical source of variability in the context of NAEP.

Identifying English Language Learners

For English language learners, there are also difficulties in identification and classification, although for somewhat different reasons. There is no legislation akin to the IDEA to provide guidance to states on identifying English language learners, and there is no universally used definition of English language learners. Hence the category includes a broad range of students whose level of fluency in English, literacy in their native language, previous academic experiences, and socioeconomic status all vary significantly. Below we present results from several analyses of state policies with regard to identification of English language learners.

Research conducted by Rivera et al. (2000) revealed that states vary considerably in the way they define English proficiency. For example, Rivera reported that 15 states base their definitions on the fairly detailed definition from the Improving America's Schools Act of 1994, that is, a limited English proficient individual is one who (Rivera et al., 2000, p. 4):

> (a) was not born in the United States or whose native language is a language other than English and comes from an environment where a language other than English is dominant; or

(b) is a Native American, or Alaska Native, or a native resident of the outlying areas and comes from an environment where a language other than English has had a significant impact on such individual's level of English proficiency; or (c) is migratory and whose native language is other than English and comes from an environment where a language other than English is dominant; and (d) who has sufficient difficulty speaking, reading, writing, or understanding the English language, and whose difficulties may deny such an individual the opportunity to learn successfully in classrooms where the language of instruction is English or to participate fully in society.

According to Rivera et al. (2000), other states use much less detailed definitions, such as "students who do not understand, speak, read or write English" (in Pennsylvania) or "students assessed as having English skills below their age appropriate grade level" (in Missouri). In addition, some states base the identification on information gathered from enrollment records, home language surveys, interviews, observations, and teacher referrals, while others identify students as English language learners from their performance on tests designed to measure "English proficiency" (National Research Council, 2000b).

More recently, the U.S. Department of Education's Office of English-language Acquisition, Language Enhancement, and Academic Achievement for Limited English Proficient Students (OELA) conducted a survey that provided some data on the variety of criteria states use for identifying students as English language learners (Kindler, 2002). Among the state education agencies responding to the survey, about 80 percent use home language surveys, teacher observation, teacher interviews, and parent information to identify students as English language learners; 60 percent use student records, student grades, informal assessments, and referrals. Most also use some type of language proficiency test. The most widely used tests are the Language Assessment Scales, the IDEA Language Proficiency Tests, and the Woodcock-Munoz Language Survey. A number of states also used results from achievement tests to identify students with limited English proficiency. The results from this survey are presented in Table 4-1.

As of 2001, most states allowed English language learners to be exempted from statewide assessments for a certain period of time (Golden and Sacks, 2001). According to Rivera, 11 states allowed a 2-year delay before including such students in testing, 21 states allowed 3 years, 2 states allowed more than 3, and 1 state had no time limit (Golden and Sacks, 2001).

Jurisdictions also differ in the amount of time they allow English language learners to receive educational supports. Some offer services for as little as one year; others for multiple years.[2] This variation can have significant implications

---

[2]Although these limits are common, researchers have found that it typically takes three to five years for English language learners to develop true oral proficiency. Academic proficiency—the capacity to use spoken and written English with sufficient complexity that one's academic performance is not impaired at all—takes longer, four to seven years on average (Hakuta et al., 1999).

TABLE 4-1 Methods States Use for Identifying English Language Learners

Methods for Identifying English Language Learners		Number of States[a]
Type of Data	Home language	50
	Parent information	48
	Teacher observation	46
	Student records	45
	Teacher interview	45
	Referral	44
	Student grades	43
	Other	32
Tests	Language proficiency tests:	51
	Language assessment scales	46
	IDEA language proficiency tests	38
	Woodcock-Munoz Language Survey	28
	Language assessment battery	13
	Basic Inventory of Natural Languages	6
	Maculaitis assessment	6
	Secondary Level English Proficiency	6
	Woodcock Language Proficiency Battery	6
	Achievement Tests:	41
	State Achievement Test	16
	Stanford	15
	ITBS	14
	CTBS	11
	Gates-MacGinitie	11
	Terra Nova	11
	Criterion Referenced Tests (CRT):	21
	State CRT	1
	NWEA Assessment	4
	District CRT/Benchmark	3
	Qualitative Reading Inventory	3
	Other CRT	5
	Other Test	19

[a]Includes states, the District of Columbia, and outlying areas (n = 54).
SOURCE: Kindler (2002, p. 9).

not only for students' academic careers, but also for the data collected about them. Jurisdictions typically do not track English language learners' progress once they stop receiving educational supports, although they may be far from fluent. Moreover, students who are no longer identified as needing educational supports would not ordinarily receive testing accommodations either.

The No Child Left Behind Act of 2001 provides a definition of English language learners that all states are to use, at least in the context of the assessments the act requires them to undertake, but this definition, too, is open to interpretation.

According to the legislation, the term "limited English proficient," when used with respect to an individual means an individual—

(a) who is aged 3 through 21;
(b) who is enrolled or preparing to enroll in an elementary or secondary school;
(c) (i) who was not born in the United States or whose native language is a language other than English;
    (ii)(I) who is a Native American or Alaska native, or a native resident of the outlying areas; and
        (II) who comes from an environment where a language other than English has had a significant impact on the individual's level of English-language proficiency; or
    (iii) who is migratory, whose native language is other than English, and who comes from an environment where a language other than English is dominant; and
(d) whose difficulties in speaking, reading, writing, or understanding the English-language may be sufficient to deny the individual—
    (i) the ability to meet the State's proficient level of achievement on State assessments described in section 1111(b)(3);
    (ii) the ability to successfully achieve in classrooms where the language of instruction is English; or
    (iii) the opportunity to participate fully in society.

Data are not yet available on how states are applying this new definition. The extent to which state policies will continue to vary remains to be seen.

Policies on Accommodation

NAEP results are also affected by the ways in which students with disabilities and English language learners are accommodated when they participate in NAEP. As was noted earlier, NAEP officials have been investigating ways of including more students in these two groups in testing, and thus the pros and cons of providing available accommodations. These decisions for NAEP are influenced by decisions made at the local level in several ways. However, like the identification procedures discussed above, policies in this area vary significantly from state to state.

In their efforts to comply with federal legislation and include these students in accountability programs, states and districts have been devising their policies without the benefit of either nationally recognized guidelines or a clear research base for overcoming many specific difficulties in assessing students with disabilities and English language learners. Not only do existing policies and procedures vary from state to state, but also they change frequently in many places as states adjust to changes in their student populations, in their testing programs, in the political climate surrounding testing, and in the evidence emerging from both research and practice. It is also important to note in this context that states' policies regarding accommodations properly depend in part on the constructs measured by specific assessments, which vary from test to test and from state to state.

Until recently, states could exclude students from their state and local testing. Now, under the requirements of the No Child Left Behind Act of 2001, states must strive to include all students with disabilities and English language learners in their accountability systems. This means that they must find a means to evaluate these students' skills in reading and math, either by including them in the standard state assessment or by providing an alternate assessment. State's inclusion and accommodation policies for the two groups of students are described below.

Accommodation Policies for Students with Disabilities

As was mentioned earlier, now that states must include nearly all students in their assessments, the importance of accommodations has grown. All states define both allowable and nonallowable practices, the latter being those that are believed to alter the construct being assessed. In general the testing accommodations for students with disabilities are based on the services and classroom accommodations that have been identified in the IEP, and the IEP is considered the authoritative guide to testing accommodations for each student who has one. Table 4-2 presents recent data on the types of accommodations that states currently allow.

Accommodation Policies for English Language Learners

In many states, the policies for including and accommodating English language learners have been derived from those established for students with disabilities (Golden and Sacks, 2001), and these have not always been clearly suited to the needs of both kinds of students. The No Child Left Behind Act has meant that far fewer English language learners can be excluded from assessments, and that accommodations and alternate assessments will be used for many students who might formerly have been excluded. The variation in policies for accommodating these students around the country is similar to that evident for students with disabilities. Table 4-3 provides recent data on the types of accommodations states currently use.

Differences Between NAEP Policies and State Policies

Since NAEP, unlike the states, is not required by law to include all students with disabilities and English language learners in their assessments, NAEP officials are free to continue to adhere to the policies they have devised for both

TABLE 4-2 Accommodations for Students with Disabilities Allowed for State Assessments and for NAEP

Type of Accommodation	Number of States That Allow the Accommodation	Allowed in NAEP
Presentation:		
Oral reading of questions	47	Yes (except for reading)
Large print	48	Yes
Braille	47	No[a]
Read aloud	46	Yes (except for reading)
Signing of directions	48	No[a]
Oral reading of directions	48	Not specified
Audio taped directions or questions	29	No
Repeating of directions	47	Yes
Explanation of directions	38	Yes
Interpretation of directions	28	Not specified
Short segment testing booklets	14	Not specified
Equipment:		
Use of magnifying glass	47	Not specified
Amplification	No info	Not specified
Light/acoustics	No info	Yes
Calculator	No info	Only on calculator use
Templates to reduce visual field	38	Not specified
Response Format:		
Use of scribe	48	Yes
Write in test booklet	44	Yes
Use template for recording answers	29	Not specified
Point to response, answer orally	41	Yes
Use sign language	42	No[a]
Use typewriter/computer/word processor	41	Yes
Use of Braille writer	42	Yes
Answers recorded on audio tape	32	No
Scheduling/Timing:		
Extended time	46	Yes
More breaks	46	Yes
Extending sessions over multiple days	37	No
Altered time of day that test is given	41	Not specified
Setting:		
Individual administration	47	Yes
Small group	47	Yes
Separate room	47	Yes
Alone in study carrel	43	Yes
At home with supervision	27	Not specified
In special education class	46	Not specified
Other:		
Out of level testing	15	No
Use of word lists or dictionaries	25	No
Spell checker	16	No

[a]Not provided by NAEP, but school, district, or state may provide after fulfilling NAEP security requirements.
SOURCES: Annual Survey of State Student Assessment Programs 2000-2001 (Council of Chief State School Officers, 2002); Available: http://nces.ed.gov/nationsreportcard/about/inclusion.asp#accom_table.

TABLE 4-3 Accommodations for English Language Learners Allowed for State Assessments and for NAEP

Accommodation	Number of States That Allow the Accommodation	Allowed in NAEP
Presentation:		
Oral reading in English	34	Yes (except for reading)
Person familiar to student administers test	36	Yes
Translation of directions	28	No
Translation of test into native language	13	No
Bilingual version of test (English and native language)	5	Yes, Spanish version of math
Oral reading in native language	18	No
Explanation of directions	32	Yes
Response Format:		
Respond in native language	10	No
Respond in native language and English	9	No
Scheduling/Timing:		
Extended time (same day)	40	Yes
More breaks	34	Yes
Extending sessions over multiple days	26	No
Setting:		
Small group	41	Yes
Separate room	40	Yes
Alone in study carrel	37	Yes
Other:		
Out of level testing	2	No
Use of word lists or dictionaries	24	Bilingual dictionary (except for reading)
Use of technology	13	Not specified

SOURCES: Annual Survey of State Student Assessment Programs 2000-2001 (Council of Chief State School Officers, 2002); Available: http://nces.ed.gov/nationsreportcard/about/inclusion.asp#accom_table.

inclusion and accommodation. The sponsors of NAEP have, however, as has been noted, been exploring modifications to these policies with the goal of increasing the participation of students in both groups. NAEP's current inclusion policy follows (http://nces.ed.gov/nationsreportcard/about/criteria.asp):

A student identified as having a disability, that is, a student with an IEP or equivalent classification, should be included in NAEP unless:

• The IEP team or equivalent group has determined that the student cannot participate in assessments such as NAEP, or
• The student's cognitive functioning is so severely impaired that he or she cannot participate, or

- The student's IEP requires that the student be tested with an accommodation that NAEP does not permit, and the student cannot demonstrate his or her knowledge of reading or mathematics without that accommodation.

A student who is identified as limited English proficient (LEP) and who is a native speaker of a language other than English should be included in NAEP unless (http://nces.ed.gov/nationsreportcard/about/criteria.asp):

- The student has received reading or mathematics instruction primarily in English for *less than 3* school years including the current year, *and*
- The student cannot demonstrate his or her knowledge of reading or mathematics in English even with an accommodation permitted by NAEP.

The phrase "less than 3 school years including the current year" means 0, 1, or 2 school years. Therefore, in applying the criteria:

- Include without any accommodation all LEP students who have received reading or mathematics instruction primarily in English for 3 years or more and those who are in their third year;
- Include without any accommodation all other LEP students who can demonstrate their knowledge of reading or mathematics without an accommodation;
- Include and provide accommodations permitted by NAEP to other LEP students who can demonstrate their knowledge of reading or mathematics only with those accommodations; and
- Exclude LEP students only if they cannot demonstrate their knowledge of reading or mathematics even with an accommodation permitted by NAEP.

The decision regarding whether any of the students identified as SD or LEP cannot be included in the assessment should be made in consultation with knowledgeable school staff. When there is doubt, the student should be included.

As for accommodations, NAEP allows some that are typically allowed on state and district assessments, but there are many used by states and districts that NAEP does not allow. For example, reading aloud of passages or questions on the reading assessment is explicitly prohibited, and alternative language versions and bilingual glossaries are not permitted on the reading assessments. Braille forms are allowed but used only if schools can provide the necessary resources to create the forms. Allowable and nonallowable accommodations for NAEP are listed in column 2 of Table 4-2 and Table 4-3.

Decisions about which of the allowed accommodations will be provided to individual students selected for a NAEP assessment are made by school authorities. In general, school authorities rely on the guidance provided in the student's IEP regarding required accommodations for students with disabilities. As has been noted, there is currently no legislation parallel to IDEA to guide decision making about accommodations for English language learners. When a student in either group requires an accommodation that is not on the approved list for NAEP, the student is generally excluded from the assessment.

While a detailed investigation of the implementation of the policies regarding inclusion and accommodation in NAEP at the school level was beyond the scope of the committee's charge, it is worth noting here that a considerable amount of responsibility for the implementation of the sampling procedure rests with school-level coordinators. Since it is clear that uniformity in this process is very important to the integrity of the sampling procedure and the accuracy of the assessment results, we raise the caution that precise instructions as to the handling of ambiguous circumstances are needed to ensure that coordinators make decisions that are consistent both with NAEP guidelines and with the decisions being made in other schools in the sample.

The committee has become aware of anecdotal reports from state officials that coordinators may not, in all cases, be completely familiar with the IEP process, with state and district accommodations policies, or with federal law regarding inclusion and accommodation; these reports also indicate that there may be instances in which the coordinators have not adhered to the NAEP guidelines. It is not clear that the oversight of this aspect of the process is adequate, or that the implementation is as uniform as it needs to be. We hope that this issue will be investigated further by the sponsors of NAEP.

REPRESENTATIVENESS OF NAEP SAMPLES

There are several complications that affect the NAEP sampling procedures for students with disabilities and English language learners. First, as noted earlier, NAEP's purpose is defined in legislation (see Section 303 of HR 3801), and the assessment is generally understood to provide results that reflect the academic proficiency of the nation's entire population of fourth, eighth, and twelfth graders. However, the target population is not precisely described in the legislation. The legislation does not provide details about the characteristics of the target population that the assessed samples must match. Indeed, the only specific points made in the legislation are that the target population should be national and should include both public and private schools.

This ambiguity creates difficulties. Although the national results presented in NAEP's reports are designed to be representative of fourth, eighth, and twelfth grade students in the nation (U.S. Department of Education National Center for Education Statistics and Institute of Education Sciences, 2003, p. 135), students with disabilities and English language learners may be excluded from NAEP sampling at two stages in the process. First, students with disabilities may be excluded because schools exclusively devoted to special education students are not included in the sampling. Second, students with disabilities and English language learners may be excluded because the test is not administered to students who, in the judgment of school personnel, cannot meaningfully participate.[3]

---

[3]That is, students with disabilities who would require an accommodation that is not allowed on NAEP or an alternate assessment, as well as English language learners who do not meet NAEP's rules for inclusion.

With regard to exclusion at the first stage, the key point is that students may be systematically excluded from the population that is sampled. Special education schools serve a wide range of students, including both students with lower levels of cognitive functioning and students with higher levels of cognitive functioning whose placement in such schools is the result of physical (e.g., visual, hearing, or motor skill impairments) or behavioral problems. Thus, there is a potential bias in the resulting estimates of performance as a consequence of this exclusion.

An additional complication arises as a result of local decision making. That is, there is another way in which the sample of students actually tested may have characteristics different from those of the target population, and it is difficult to estimate the extent of this divergence. As we have seen, the decisions made by school personnel in identifying students as having disabilities or being English language learners vary both within states and across states, but there is no way to measure this variance or its effect on the sample. Nevertheless, it is very likely that students are excluded from NAEP according to criteria that are not uniform. If this is so, statistical "noise" is introduced into inferences that are based on comparisons of performance across states.

Results from the 2002 administration of the NAEP reading assessment indicated that of all students nationwide selected for the sample, 6 percent were excluded from participation at the fourth grade level for some reason. Exclusion was somewhat less frequent for older students: 5 percent at the eighth grade level and 4 percent at the twelfth grade level (U.S. Department of Education, National Center for Education Statistics, and Institute of Education Sciences, 2003, pp. 151-152). Although certain students selected for inclusion are not ultimately assessed in NAEP, those who do not participate are still accounted for. That is, students selected for a NAEP sample are placed into three categories: regular participation, participation with accommodations, and excluded. If the argument can be made that the excluded category reflects students who could not meaningfully participate in the assessment, including those who receive their education in special education schools, then NAEP results can be understood to reflect the academic achievement of all students who can be assessed "in a valid and reliable manner," using tools currently available. However, if the excluded category includes students who might have been able to participate meaningfully but who were excluded because of incorrect or inconsistent applications of the guidelines, or because a needed, appropriate accommodation was not permitted or available, then inferences about the generalizability of NAEP results to the full population of the nation's students are compromised.

An Attempt to Compare the Composition of a NAEP Sample with National Demographics

The committee was concerned about the extent to which the samples of students included in NAEP are representative of the numbers of students with disabilities and English language learners nationwide. We explored this issue by attempting to compile data with which to compare the characteristics of NAEP's samples to the characteristics of the nation's population of students with disabilities and English language learners. Table 4-4 presents the results of this attempt.

For this table, data on the total enrollment in public schools (see row 7) were obtained from the NCES Common Core of Data survey, Table 38 (http://nces.ed.gov/programs/digest/d02/tables/PDF/table38.pdf); this is the number of students enrolled in the 50 states, the District of Columbia, and outlying areas in the specified grade for the 2000-2001 school year. The number of students with disabilities (column 1, row 1) was obtained from the 24th Annual Report to

TABLE 4-4 Comparisons of the Percentages of Students with Disabilities and English Language Learners in the United States[a] for the 2000-2001 School Year with Those in the NAEP Samples for 2002 Reading and 2003 Mathematics

	(1) Students with Disabilities		(2) English Language Learners	
	Fourth Graders/ 9-Year-Olds	Eighth Graders/ 13-Year-Olds	Fourth Graders	Eighth Graders
National Data				
(1) Number in United States	522,370[b]	501,008[b]	169,421[c]	108,994[c]
(2) Percentage of Total U.S. Enrollment	14.1%[d]	14.2%[e]	4.6%	3.1%
Percentages of NAEP Sample[f]				
(3) *Identified* for 2002 Reading	12%	12%	8%	6%
(4) *Assessed* in 2002 Reading	7%	8%	6%	4%
(5) *Identified* for 2003 Math	13%	13%	10%	6%
(6) *Assessed* in 2003 Math	10%	10%	8%	5%

(7) Total enrollment in United States: fourth grade = 3,707,931; eighth grade = 3,432,370

[a]Based on data for the 50 states, the District of Columbia, and outlying areas.
[b]Counts of students with disabilities in the United States are by age.
[c]Counts of English language learners in the United States are by grade.
[d]Number of students with disabilities age 9 divided by total number of enrolled fourth graders.
[e]Number of students with disabilities age 13 divided by total number of enrolled eighth graders.
[f]All percentages in NAEP are by grade level.
SOURCES: Kindler (2002); NAEP 2003 Mathematics Report available http://nces.ed.gov/nationsreportcard/mathematics/results2003/acc-permitted-natl-yes.asp; NCES Common Core of Data Survey available http://nces.ed.gov/programs/digest/d02/tables/PDF/table 38.pdf; U.S. Department of Education (2002), Table AA8; U.S. Department of Education National Center for Education Statistics and Institute of Education Sciences (2003).

Congress, Table AA8, and is the number of children served under the IDEA during the 2000-2001 school year in the United States and outlying areas; these data are reported by age, not grade, so the counts for 9-year-olds and 13-year-olds were used (U.S. Department of Education, 2002). The percentage of students with disabilities in the nation (column 1, row 2) was calculated by dividing the counts in row 1 by the appropriate totals in row 7. The counts of English language learners were obtained from Kindler (2002) and are the number of students (column 2, row 1) enrolled in the specified grade in the United States and outlying areas during the 2000-2001 school year. The percentage of English language learners in the nation (column 2, row 2) was calculated by dividing the counts in row 1 by the appropriate totals in row 7. The weighted percentages[4] of the NAEP sample, which appear in rows 3 through 8, were obtained from the NAEP's 2002 Reading Report (see Table 3-3) and NAEP's 2003 Mathematics Report (http://nces.ed.gov/nationsreportcard/mathematics/results2003/acc-permitted-natl-yes.asp). Rows 3 and 5 show the percentage of the NAEP sample *identified* (by school officials) as students with disabilities or English language learners; rows 4 and 6 show the percentage of the NAEP sample of students *assessed* who had disabilities or were English language learners.

At a first glance, these data suggest that the NAEP sampling underrepresents the numbers of students with disabilities and slightly overrepresents the numbers of English language learners. However, interpretation of these data is complicated by the fact that they are not directly comparable. For example, the counts for students with disabilities are for age group, not grade level. The national demographics on students with disabilities and English language learners include counts of students for outlying areas (American Samoa, Guam, Northern Marianas, Puerto Rico, Virgin Islands), which are not all always included in the NAEP sample, and the way in which the data were reported would not allow disentangling these numbers for all of the columns on this table.[5]

Furthermore, the differences in the estimated proportions of students with disabilities and English language learners sampled in NAEP and existing in the United States could be attributable to differences in the way students are counted, the way the data are reported, or both; neither source for the estimated proportions should be considered infallible. In addition, the most current national data available at the time this report was being prepared were for a different school

---

[4]Percentages are weighted according to sampling weights determined as part of NAEP's sampling procedures. These "weighted percentages" are the percentages that appear in NAEP reports.

[5]While grade level counts for the entire enrollment and for students with disabilities were available for various combinations of the 50 states, the District of Columbia, Department of Defense schools, outlying areas, and Bureau of Land Management schools, grade-level counts for English language learners were available only for the 50 states, the District of Columbia, and outlying areas.

year (2000-2001) than the one in which the NAEP assessment occurred (2001-2002). Nevertheless, we include this information for two reasons. One is that we strongly believe that attempts should be made to evaluate the extent to which NAEP samples are representative of the students with disabilities and English language learners nationwide. Second, we call attention to the deficiencies in the existing data sources and the consequent difficulties in making such comparisons.

We further note that while national data may be useful in evaluating the representativeness of national NAEP results, state-level demographics would be needed to evaluate the representativeness of the state NAEP results. Tables 3-4 and 3-5 presented data by state on the percentages of students with disabilities and English language learners, respectively, who participated in NAEP's 1998 and 2002 reading assessments. We attempted to evaluate the representativeness of the state samples with respect to the two groups of students but were unable to obtain all of the necessary data. We were able to obtain data on the percentages of students with disabilities who are age 9 and age 13 for each state, but again these data were not available by grade level. We were not able to obtain grade-level or age-level data by states for English language learners. The data we were able to obtain are presented in Table 4-5.

In the table, state-level enrollment counts for fourth and eighth grades (columns 2 and 6) were obtained from Table 38 of NCES's Common Core of Data surveys (http://nces.ed.gov/programs/digest/d02/tables.dt038.asp). Counts of students with disabilities by state (columns 3 and 7) were obtained from the 24th Annual Report to Congress, Table AA8 (U.S. Department of Education, 2002). Percentages (columns 4 and 8) were calculated by dividing column 3 by column 2 and column 7 by column 6. The percentages in column 5 were taken from Table 3-4 and are the percentages of students with disabilities identified by school officials and assessed for the fourth grade 2002 NAEP Reading Assessment. Likewise, the percentages in column 9 were obtained from NAEP's report of the percent of students with disabilities identified by school officials and assessed for the eighth grade 2002 NAEP Reading Assessment (http://nces.ed.gov/nationsreportcard/reading/results2002/acc-sd-g8.asp).

Thus the committee found that it was not possible to compare the proportions of students with disabilities and English language learners in NAEP samples with their incidence in the population at large. Local, state, and federal agencies do not produce the kinds of comparable data that would make these comparisons possible at the national level. Moreover, although it would also be important to compare state NAEP results with the proportions of students with disabilities and English language learners in the respective state populations, those comparisons are also, by and large, not possible. As was discussed earlier, states in many cases collect the desired data but do not present them in a way that makes it possible to compare them with state NAEP results or to compile them across states.

TABLE 4-5 Comparisons of the Percentages of Students with Disabilities in the United States for the 2000-2001 School Year with Those in the Sample for NAEP's 2002 Reading Assessment in Fourth and Eighth Grade

(1) State	Fourth Graders/9-Year-Olds				Eighth Graders/13-Year-Olds			
	(2) Total Enrollment[a]	Students with Disabilities[b]		(5) Percent (Identified) and Assessed in NAEP[a]	(6) Total Enrollment[a]	Students with Disabilities[b]		(9) Percentage (Identified) and Assessed in NAEP[a]
		(3) N	(4) Percent[c]			(7) N	(8) Percent[d]	
Alabama	59,749	7,976	13.3	(13) 11	56,951	8,129	14.3	(13) 11
Alaska	10,646	1,553	14.6	Not available	10,377	1,398	13.5	(15) 14
Arizona	72,295	8,173	11.3	(11) 7	65,526	8,132	12.4	(11) 9
Arkansas	35,724	4,178	11.7	(12) 7	34,873	4,566	13.1	(15) 13
California	489,043	55,266	11.3	(7) 4	441,877	51,888	11.7	(11) 9
Colorado	57,056	6,511	11.4	Not available	55,386	6,188	11.2	(12) 10
Connecticut	44,682	5,624	12.6	(13) 9	42,597	6,182	14.5	(14) 11
Delaware	8,848	1,404	15.9	(15) 8	9,075	1,291	14.2	(16) 8
District of Columbia	5,830	934	16	14 (7)	3,371	869	25.8	(16) 11
Florida	194,320	30,783	15.8	(17) 13	185,663	28,953	15.6	(14) 12
Georgia	116,678	14,948	12.8	(10) 7	109,124	13,406	12.3	(11) 10
Hawaii	15,291	1,882	12.3	(12) 8	13,424	1,914	14.3	(16) 13
Idaho	18,964	2,486	13.1	(13) 9	19,045	2,138	11.2	(10) 10
Illinois	160,495	25,335	15.8	(13) 9	149,045	22,630	15.2	(15) 12
Indiana	79,738	13,829	17.3	(12) 8	73,888	11,256	15.2	(14) 11
Iowa	36,448	5,708	15.7	(15) 8	36,458	6,034	16.6	(16) 14
Kansas	35,165	4,910	14	(14) 10	36,085	4,456	12.3	(13) 11

continued

Kentucky	50,899	7,017	13.8	(11) 4	48,938	6,526	13.3	(13) 9
Louisiana	63,884	7,174	11.2	(19) 8	61,997	7,568	12.2	(16) 11
Maine	16,121	2,810	17.4	(16) 10	17,035	2,831	16.6	(16) 12
Maryland	69,279	9,167	13.2	(12) 6	64,647	9,331	14.4	(14) 10
Massachusetts	78,287	12,213	15.6	(16) 12	74,527	13,376	17.9	(16) 14
Michigan	130,886	18,530	14.2	(11) 4	123,080	17,483	14.2	(13) 8
Minnesota	63,334	8,758	13.8	(13) 10	66,254	8,526	12.9	(13) 11
Mississippi	40,177	4,479	11.1	(7) 3	36,588	4,226	11.6	(9) 4
Missouri	71,208	11,540	16.2	(15) 7	68,717	11,098	16.2	(15) 12
Montana	11,682	1,653	14.1	(13) 8	12,517	1,524	12.2	(12) 10
Nebraska	21,357	3,793	17.8	(18) 4	21,864	3,339	15.3	(14) 11
Nevada	28,616	3,349	11.7	(12) 7	25,327	2,995	11.8	(12) 10
New Hampshire	16,852	2,306	13.7	Not available	17,209	2,600	15.1	(19) 15
New Jersey	100,622	18,696	18.6	Not available	92,094	16,958	18.4	(19) 14
New Mexico	25,493	3,913	15.3	(15) 9	24,870	4,394	17.7	(20) 18
New York	217,881	33,689	15.5	(14) 8	203,482	33,273	16.4	(16) 12
North Carolina	105,105	15,421	14.7	(17) 6	99,295	13,483	13.6	(16) 12
North Dakota	7,982	1,127	14.1	(16) 11	8,651	1,023	11.8	(14) 13
Ohio	143,373	19,400	13.5	(13) 8	139,740	18,727	13.4	(13) 8
Oklahoma	47,064	7,147	15.2	(17) 13	46,276	6,785	14.7	(16) 14
Oregon	43,436	6,774	15.6	(16) 10	42,364	6,128	14.5	(14) 12
Pennsylvania	142,366	19,434	13.7	(13) 9	143,638	19,247	13.4	(14) 13
Rhode Island	12,490	2,581	20.7	(19) 15	11,750	2,469	21	(20) 17
South Carolina	54,468	8,865	16.3	(16) 11	53,259	7,853	14.7	(15) 8
South Dakota	9,583	1,489	15.5	(11) 8	10,303	1,055	10.2	(11) 9
Tennessee	73,373	10,046	13.7	(11) 8	66,429	9,675	14.6	(14(12)
Texas	313,731	38,906	12.4	(14) 6	304,419	41,946	13.8	(15) 9
Utah	35,910	4,652	13	(12) 7	34,579	3,831	11.1	(11) 9
Vermont	7,736	1,035	13.4	(13) 9	8,005	1,174	14.7	(17) 15

82

TABLE 4-5 Continued

(1) State	Fourth Graders/9-Year-Olds				Eighth Graders/13-Year-Olds			
	(2) Total Enrollment[a]	(3) N Students with Disabilities[b]	(4) Percent[c]	(5) Percent (Identified) and Assessed in NAEP[a]	(6) Total Enrollment[a]	(7) N Students with Disabilities[b]	(8) Percent[d]	(9) Percentage (Identified) and Assessed in NAEP[a]
Virginia	92,073	13,860	15.1	(14) 6	87,455	12,933	14.8	(15) 9
Washington	78,505	10,340	13.2	(13) 9	77,160	8,970	11.6	(13) 11
West Virginia	21,995	4,038	18.4	(15) 5	21,902	3,753	17.1	(16) 13
Wisconsin	64,455	9,080	14.1	(13) 8	67,950	9,441	13.9	(15) 13
Wyoming	6,736	1,005	14.9	(14) 2	7,284	945	13	(15) 14

[a]Counts and percentages are by grade level.
[b]Counts and percentages are by age.
[c]Number of students with disabilities age 9 divided by total number of enrolled fourth graders.
[d]Number of students with disabilities age 13 divided by total number of enrolled eighth graders.

SOURCES: NCES Common Core of Data Survey available http://nces.ed.gov/programs/digest/d02/tables/PDF/table 38.pdf; U.S. Department of Education (2002),Table AA8; U.S. Department of Education National Center for Education Statistics and Institute of Education Sciences (2003).

FINDINGS AND RECOMMENDATIONS

Our review of policies and procedures for identifying students with disabilities and English language learners and for including and accommodating these students in NAEP and other large-scale assessments has revealed a large amount of variability both among and within states and between the states and NAEP. We recognize that the task of standardizing inclusion and accommodation policies is not a small one, but in our judgment improvements can be made.

Greater uniformity in these procedures is important for several reasons. First, in the context of NAEP, the integrity of NAEP samples, and consequently the accuracy of its data, depend on the consistency with which students are identified as students with disabilities or as English language learners, as well as on the consistency with which they are included in and accommodated for NAEP testing around the country. The integrity of the samples is of paramount importance for data regarding students with disabilities and English language learners, but it also affects the validity of NAEP data about the population as a whole and other subgroups as well.

At the same time there exists the possibility that greater attention to the data regarding students with disabilities and English language learners provided by NAEP, and the factors that complicate interpretation of these data, may raise difficult questions for NAEP. To date, litigation concerning accommodations has primarily been related to so-called high-stakes tests, whose results are used in decisions about promotion, graduation, and placement for individual students. There have been no legal challenges to NAEP because its results are not used to make high-stakes decisions. However, as NAEP continues to be viewed as a tool for evaluating how the nation's students are progressing in the context of the goals for the No Child Left Behind Act, its conclusion and accommodation policies may need to be sharpened and aligned with those of state assessment systems.

In the committee's view, it is important to know the extent to which the percentages in the NAEP reports correspond to the percentages of students with disabilities and English language learners reported in other sources. The committee believes that many states are undertaking additional efforts at collecting such data, partly in response to the requirements of such legislation as the No Child Left Behind Act of 2001. We encourage all parties (NAEP as well as state and federal agencies) to collect and compile such data so that the desired comparisons can be made.

Specifically, the committee takes note of the following circumstances:

FINDING 4-1: Decision making regarding the inclusion or exclusion of students and the use of accommodations for NAEP is controlled at the school level. There is variability in the way these decisions are made, both across schools within a state and across states.

FINDING 4-2: The target population for NAEP assessments is not clearly defined. It is not clear to whom the results are intended to generalize.

FINDING 4-3: The extent to which the demographic estimates in NAEP reports compare with the actual proportions of students with disabilities and English language learners is not known; in part, this is the result of deficiencies in the national and state-level demographic data that are available.

Our review of these circumstances leads us to make the following recommendations:

RECOMMENDATION 4-1: NAEP officials should:

- review the criteria for inclusion and accommodation of students with disabilities and English language learners in NAEP in light of federal guidelines;
- clarify, elaborate, and revise their criteria as needed; and
- standardize the implementation of these criteria at the school level.

RECOMMENDATION 4-2: NAEP officials should work with state assessment directors to review the policies regarding inclusion and accommodation in NAEP assessments and work toward greater consistency between NAEP and state assessment procedures.

RECOMMENDATION 4-3: NAEP should more clearly define the characteristics of the population of students to whom the results are intended to generalize. This definition should serve as a guide for decision making and the formulation of regulations regarding inclusion, exclusion, and reporting.

RECOMMENDATION 4-4: NAEP officials should evaluate the extent to which their estimates of the percentages of students with disabilities and English language learners in a state are comparable to similar data collected and reported by states to the extent feasible given the data that are available. Differences should be investigated to determine the causes.

In addition to those four recommendations to NAEP officials, we also recommend that:

RECOMMENDATION 4-5: Efforts should be made to improve the availability of data about students with disabilities and English language learners. State-level data are needed that report the total number of English language learners and students with disabilities by grade level in the state. This information should be compiled in a way that allows comparisons to be made across states and should be made readily accessible.

5

Available Research on the Effects of Accommodations on Validity

From the perspective of score interpretation, the purpose of testing accommodations is to reduce the dependence of test scores on factors that are irrelevant to the construct that is being assessed. As Haertel (2003, p. 11) noted:

> Ideally, the accommodation would eliminate some particular impediment faced by a given examinee, so that the accommodated administration for that examinee was equivalent to a standard accommodation for a typical examinee in all other respects. The score earned by the accommodated examinee would then be interpreted as conveying the same information with respect to the intended construct as a score obtained under standard administration conditions.

Thus in investigating the validity of inferences based on accommodated testing there are two paramount questions: Do the accommodated and unaccommodated versions of the test measure the same construct? If so, are they equivalent in difficulty and precision? Evidence that the answers to both questions is yes constitutes support for considering the two versions equivalent.

In the past several years, there have been numerous calls for research into accommodations for students with disabilities and English language learners. The National Research Council (NRC) (1999a), for example, called for a research agenda that includes studies of "the need for particular types of accommodations and the adequacy and appropriateness of accommodations applied to various categories of students with disabilities and English-language learners" and "the validity of different types of accommodations" (National Research Council, 1999a, pp. 110-111). Participants at an NRC workshop on reporting test results for students with disabilities and English language learners outlined a full agenda of research into the effects of accommodations (National Research Council, 2002a). Two different NRC committees that addressed the educational needs and concerns of students with disabilities (National Research Council, 1997a) and English language learners (National Research Council, 2000b) both recommended programs of research aimed at investigating the performance of these groups in large-scale standardized assessments.

A substantial amount of useful and interesting research is already available on the effects of accommodations on test performance, and several extensive reviews of this literature have been conducted. The effects of accommodations on test performance have been reviewed by Chiu and Pearson (1999); Tindal and Fuchs (2000); and Thompson et al. (2002). However, much of the existing research focuses on whether or not the accommodation had an effect on performance and, in some cases, on whether the effect was different for students with and without disabilities. Little of the available research directly addresses the validity of inferences made from the results of accommodated assessments, yet it is this second kind of research that could really assist policy makers and others in making decisions about accommodations. In this chapter, we review the available research regarding accommodations and outline the current methods of conducting validity research. In Chapter 6 we present the committee's view of the way the validity of inferences based on accommodated assessments can best be evaluated.

EFFECTS OF ACCOMMODATIONS AND THE INTERACTION HYPOTHESIS

The committee commissioned a review and critique of the available research on the effects of test accommodations on the performance of students with disabilities and English language learners in order to gauge both any discernible trends in this research and the thoroughness with which the issues have been studied. This review was conducted by Sireci et al. (2003).

The authors were asked to review and critically evaluate the literature on test accommodations, focusing on empirical studies that examined the effects of accommodations on individuals' test performance. The authors began their review with the articles summarized in the NRC's workshop report (National Research Council, 2002a), additional articles provided by NRC staff, and questions raised about the studies during the workshop. They supplemented the lists provided by searching two electronic databases, ERIC and PsychInfo, and the web sites of the Center for Research on Evaluation, Standards, and Student Testing (CRESST) and the National Center on Educational Outcomes (NCEO). They also queried researchers whose work was frequently cited, sent the authors the list of citations they had, and asked the authors to forward any additional studies. Included in the review were studies conducted between 1990 and December of 2002; the ending time was specified to ensure that the literature review would be ready in time for the committee's first meeting.

The committee asked the authors to consider the research findings in light of the criterion, often referred to as the "interaction hypothesis" that is commonly used for judging the validity of accommodations, that is, the assumption that effective test accommodations will improve test scores for the students who need the accommodation but not for the students who do not need the accommodation. As Shepard et al. (1998) explained it, if accommodations are working as intended, there should be an interaction between educational status (students with disabilities and students without disabilities) and accommodation conditions (accommodated and unaccommodated). The accommodation should improve the average score for the students for whom it was designed (students with disabilities or English language learners) but should have little or no effect on the average score for the others (students without disabilities or native English speakers). If an accommodation improves the performance of both groups, then offering it only to certain students (students with disabilities or English language learners) is unfair.

Figure 5-1 is a visual depiction of the 2 × 2 experimental design used to test for this interaction effect. An interaction effect would be said to exist if the mean score for examinees in group C were higher than the mean score for group A, and the mean scores for groups B and D were similar.

The use of this interaction hypothesis for judging the validity of scores from accommodated administrations has, however, been called into question. In particular, questions have been raised about whether the finding of score improvements for the students who ostensibly did not need accommodations (from cell B to cell D) should invalidate the accommodation (National Research Council, 2002a, pp. 74-75). For example, if both native English speakers and English language learners benefit from a plain-language accommodation, does that mean that the scores are not valid for English language learners who received this accommodation?

There are also questions about whether the finding of score improvements

	Group Identified as Needing Accommodation	Group Identified as Not Needing Accommodation
Unaccommodated	A	B
Accommodated	C	D

FIGURE 5-1 Depiction of the interaction hypothesis.

associated with the use of an accommodation is sufficient to conclude that an accommodation results in valid scores for the experimental group. At the heart of this latter question is the issue of the comparability of inferences made about scores obtained under different conditions.

Sireci and his colleagues were given criteria for including a study in their review, specifically that the study should examine the effects of test accommodations on test performance and should involve empirical analyses. The authors found that while the literature on test accommodations is "vast and passionate," with some authors arguing against accommodations on the grounds that they are unfair and others arguing in favor of them, only a subset of the literature explicitly addressed the effects of accommodations on performance using empirical analyses. The authors initially identified more than 150 studies that pertained to test accommodations; of these, however, only 46 actually focused on test accommodations and only 38 involved empirical analyses.

They classified the studies as experimental, quasi-experimental, or non-experimental. A study was classified as using an experimental design if the test administration condition (accommodated or standard) was manipulated and examinees were randomly assigned to the condition. Studies were classified as quasi-experimental if the test administration condition was manipulated but examinees were not randomly assigned to conditions. Nonexperimental studies included ex post facto studies that compared the results of students who took a test with an accommodation with those of students who took a standard version of the test and studies that looked at differences across standard and accommodated administrations for the same (self-selected) group of students.

Research on the Effects of Accommodations on the
Test Performance of Students with Disabilities

With regard to students with disabilities, Sireci et al. (2003) found 26 studies that met their criteria for inclusion in the review. The disability most frequently studied was learning disabilities, while the two accommodations most frequently studied were extended time (12 studies) and oral presentation (22 studies). Table 5-1 lists the studies that used an experimental design and provides a brief description of the findings; Table 5-2 provides similar information for studies that used quasi-experimental or nonexperimental designs. The authors summarized the findings from these studies this way (p. 48):

> One thing that is clear from our review is that there are no unequivocal conclusions that can be drawn regarding the effects, in general, of accommodations on students' test performance. The literature is clear that accommodations and students are both heterogeneous. It is also clear that the interaction hypothesis, as it is typically described, is on shaky ground. Students without disabilities typically benefit from accommodations, particularly the accommodation of extended time.

Research on the Effects of Accommodations on the Test Performance of English Language Learners

With regard to research on the effects of accommodations on test performance for English language learners, Sireci et al. (2003) found only 12 studies that met their criteria for inclusion in the review. Table 5-3 provides a list of the studies included in their review; those that are listed as using either a between-group design or a within-group design were considered to be experimental studies. The most common accommodations studied were linguistic modification, provision of a dictionary or bilingual dictionary, provision of dual-language booklets, extended time, and oral administration. Most studies examined the effects of multiple accommodations.

Sireci et al. reported that research on the effects of linguistic modification has produced mixed results. For example, they cite a study by Abedi, Hofstetter et al. (2001) in which the authors claimed that this accommodation was the most effective in reducing the score gap between English language learners and native English speakers. However, Sireci et al. (2003, p. 65) point out that in this study, "the gap was narrowed because native English speakers scored worse on the linguistically modified test, not because the English language learners performed substantially better." In addition, in a study by Abedi (2001a), significant, but small, gains were noted for eighth grade students but not for fourth grade students. Sireci et al. point out that Abedi explained this finding by hypothesizing that "With an increase in grade level, more complex language may interfere with content-based assessment" (p. 13) and "in earlier grades, language may not be as great a hurdle as it is in the later grades" (p. 14).

With regard to research on other accommodations provided to English language learners, Sireci et al. noted that providing English language learners with customized dictionaries or glossaries seemed to improve their performance (e.g., Abedi, Lord, Boscardin, and Miyoshi, 2000). The one study available on dual-language test booklets revealed no gains.

Overall Findings from the Literature Review

From their review of 38 studies that involved empirical analysis, Sireci et al. concluded that, in general, all student groups (students with disabilities, English language learners, and general education students) had score gains under accommodated conditions. While the literature review did not provide unequivocal support for interpreting accommodated scores as both valid and equivalent to unaccommodated scores, it did find that many accommodations had "positive, construct-valid effects for certain groups of students" (p. 68).

The reviewed studies focused on the issue of whether accommodations led to score increases, and whether the increases were greater for the targeted groups than for other test-takers. Evaluation of this interaction hypothesis has been cen-

TABLE 5-1 Summary of Experimental Studies on Students with Disabilities

Study	Characteristics of Sample	Accommodations	Design	Results	Interaction Detected[a]
McKevitt, Marquart, Mroch, Schulte, Elliott, and Kratochwill (2000)	Students with disabilities	Extra time, oral, encouragement, "packages"	Single-subject alternating treatment design	Greater gains for students with disabilities	Yes
Elliot, Kratochwill, and McKevitt (2001)	Students with disabilities	Encouragement, extra time, individual administration, various oral, spelling assistance, mark to maintain place, manipulatives	Single-subject alternating treatment design	Moderate to large improvement for students with disabilities	Yes
Runyan (1991)	Students with learning disabilities	Extra time	Between-groups design	Greater gains for students with disabilities	Yes
Zuriff (2000)	Students with learning disabilities	Extra time	Five different studies	Gains for both students with and without disabilities	No
Fuchs, Fuchs, Eaton, Hamlett, Binkley, and Crouch (2000)	Students with learning disabilities	Extra time, large print, student reads aloud	Between-groups design	Read aloud benefited students with learning disabilities but not others	Yes
Weston (2002)	Students with disabilities	Oral	Within- and between-groups design	Greater gains for students with disabilities	Yes
Tindal, Heath, Hollenbeck, Almond, and Harniss (1998)	Students with disabilities	Oral	Within- and between-groups design	Significant gains for students with disabilities only	Yes

Johnson (2000)	Students with disabilities	Oral	Between-groups design	Greater gains for students with disabilities	Partial
Kosciolek and Ysseldyke (2000)	Students with disabilities	Oral	Within- and between-groups design	No gains	No
Meloy, Deville, and Frisbie (2000)	Students with disabilities	Oral	Within- and between-groups design	Similar gains for students with and without disabilities	No
Brown and Augustine (2001)	Students with disabilities	Screen reading	Within- and between-groups design	No gains	No
Tindal, Anderson, Helwig, Miller, and Glasgow (1998)	Students with disabilities	Simplified English	Unclear	No gains	No
Fuchs, Fuchs, Eaton, Hamlett, and Karns (2000)	Students with learning disabilities	Calculators, extra time, reading aloud, transcription, teacher selected	Between-groups design	Differential benefit on constructed response items	Partial
Walz, Albus, Thompson, and Thurlow (2000)	Students with disabilities	Multiday/session	Within- and between-groups design	No gains for students with disabilities	No

[a]As portrayed in Figure 5-1.

TABLE 5-2 Summary of Quasi-experimental and Nonexperimental Studies on Students with Disabilities

Study	Characteristics of Sample	Accommodations	Design	Selected Findings
Cahalan, Mandinach, and Camara (2002)	Students with learning disabilities	Extended time	Ex post facto	Predictive validity was lower for learning disabled students, especially for males
Camara, Copeland, and Rothchild (1998)	Students with learning disabilities	Extended time	Ex post facto	Score gains for learning disabled retesters with extended time were three times greater than for standard retesters
Huesman and Frisbie (2000)	Students with disabilities	Extra time	Quasi-experimental	Score gains for students with learning disabilities but not for those without
Ziomeck and Andrews (1998)	Students with disabilities	Extra time	Ex post facto	Score gains for learning disabled retesters with extended time were three times greater than for standard retesters
Schulte, Elliot, and Kratochwill (2001)	Students with disabilities	Extra time, oral	Ex post facto	Students with disabilities improved more between unaccommodated and accommodated conditions (medium effect size; 0.40 to 0.80.) than those without disabilities (small effect size; less than 0.40). No differences on constructed response items
Braun, Ragosta, and Kaplan (1986)	Students with disabilities	Various	Ex post facto	Predictive validity was similar across accommodated and unaccommodated tests; slightly lower for learning disabled
Koretz and Hamilton (2000)	Students with disabilities	Various	Ex post facto	Students with disabilities performed lower than those without and differences increased with grade level. No consistent relations found between test item formats for students with disabilities

Study	Population	Accommodation	Design	Findings
Koretz and Hamilton (2001)	Students with disabilities	Various	Ex post facto	Accommodations narrowed gap more on constructed response items
Helwig and Tindal (2003)	Students with disabilities	Oral	Ex post facto	Teachers were not accurate in determining who would benefit from accommodation
McKevitt and Elliot (in press)	Students with disabilities	Oral	Ex post facto	No significant effect size differences between accommodated and unaccommodated conditions for either group
Johnson, Kimball, Brown, and Anderson (2001)	Students with disabilities	English, visual, and native language dictionaries, scribes, large print, Braille, oral	Ex post facto	Students with disabilities scored lower than those without. Accommodations did not result in an unfair advantage to special education students
Zurcher and Bryant (2001)	Students with disabilities	Not specific	Quasi-experimental	No significant gains

TABLE 5-3 Summary of Quasi-experimental and Nonexperimental Studies on English Language Learners

Study	Accommodations	Design	Results	Interaction Detected[a]
Abedi (2001b)	Simplified English, bilingual glossary, customized dictionary	Between-groups design	No effects at fourth grade. Small gain for simplified English in eighth grade	Only for eighth grade sample
Abedi, Hofstetter, Baker, and Lord (2001)[b]	Simplified English, glossary, extra time, extra time + glossary	Between-groups design	Extra time w/ and w/out glossary helped all students; simplified English narrowed the score gap between groups	No
Abedi and Lord (2001)	Simplified English	Between-groups design	Small, but insignificant gains	No
Abedi, Lord, Boscardin, and Miyoshi (2000)	English dictionary, English glosses, Spanish translation	Between-groups design	English language learner gains assoc. with dictionary; no gains for others	Yes
Abedi, Lord, and Hofstetter (1998)	Linguistic modification, Spanish translation	Between-groups design	Language modification helped all students improve scores; performance on translated version depended on language of instruction	No
Rivera and Stansfield (2001)	Linguistic modification of test	Between-groups design	No differences for non-English language learners	No
Albus, Bielinski, Thurlow, and Liu (2001)	Dictionary	Within-and between-groups design	No effect on validity; no significant overall gain for English language learners	No

Study	Accommodation	Design	Outcome	
Abedi, Courtney, Mirocha, Leon, and Goldberg (2001)	Dictionary, bilingual dictionary, linguistic modification of the test, extended time	Between-groups design	Gains for English language learners under dictionary conditions	Yes
Shepard, Taylor, and Betebenner (1998)	Various	Ex post facto	Gains for both English language learners and others	Partial
Anderson, Liu, Swierzbin, Thurlow, and Bielinski (2000)	Dual-language booklet	Within- and between-groups design	No gains	No
Garcia et al. (2000)	Dual-language booklet	Quasi-experimental	N/A	N/A
Castellon-Wellington, (1999)	Extended time, oral	Quasi-experimental	No gains	No
Hafner (2001)	Extended time, oral directions	Quasi-experimental	Score gains for both English language learners and others	Unable to determine

[a]As portrayed in Figure 5-1.

[b]Results from this study also appeared in another publication: Abedi, Lord, Hofstetter and Baker (2000). The 2000 publication included a confirmatory factor analysis to evaluate the structural equivalence of reading and math tests for English language learners and native English speakers. The correlation between reading and math was higher for English language learners.

tral to much research on testing accommodations. Sireci et al., however, suggest a less stringent form of the hypothesis that stipulates that scores for targeted groups should improve *more than* scores of other test-takers. Although the results of investigating the interaction hypothesis (in either of its forms) are clearly useful in assessing the effectiveness of an accommodation, they cannot confirm that it yields valid score interpretations because they do not permit any determination of whether the accommodated and standard versions of the test are tapping the same constructs and whether they are equal in difficulty. Evidence that satisfies the interaction hypothesis criterion therefore does not constitute a sufficient justification for the use of an accommodation.

As an illustration of the fact that the detection of an interaction is not evidence that the accommodated score is a more valid measure of the construct in question, consider the following example. Suppose that all students in a class take a spelling test in which they must write down words after hearing them read aloud. A week later, they take a second spelling test of equivalent difficulty. This time, test-takers are told that they can request a dictionary[1] to use during the test. Suppose that this accommodation is found to improve the scores of English language learners but not those of students who are native English speakers. Proponents of the interaction hypothesis would say that this finding justifies the use of the accommodation. In reality, however, nothing in these results supports the claim that the accommodated scores are more valid measures of spelling ability. In fact, logic suggests in this case that the accommodated version of the test measures a skill that is quite different from the intended one.

The fact that the accommodation affects English language learners and native English speakers differently may have any number of explanations. Native English speakers may have felt more reluctant to request a dictionary or been less likely to take the trouble to use one. Alternatively, they may have been close to their maximum performance on the first test and were not able to demonstrate substantial gains on the second test. Without some external evidence (such as an independent measure of spelling ability or, at least, of some type of verbal skill), no conclusion can be drawn about the validity of inferences from the accommodated scores relative to inferences from the scores obtained under standard administration.

CURRENT VALIDITY RESEARCH

How, then, can it be determined whether scores earned through accommodated and standard administrations are equivalent in meaning? Simply comparing

---

[1]We recognize that use of a dictionary as an accommodation for a spelling test would typically not be allowed since it would interfere with measurement of the intended construct; however, we use this example here to demonstrate our point about the lack of logic associated with the interaction hypothesis as a criterion for validity.

score distributions for students who took the test under accommodated and standard conditions is clearly insufficient, since these two groups are drawn from different student populations. To compare the meanings of the two types of scores, it is necessary to obtain other information on the construct of interest by means of measures external to the test and to examine the relationship between the accommodated and unaccommodated scores and these external variables. In order for the two scores to be considered equivalent, the relationship between the test score and these criterion variables should be the same for both types of scores.

In the area of admissions testing, in which there is some agreement on the appropriate criterion variable, some research of this kind has been conducted. At the recommendation of a National Research Council study panel, a four-year research program was undertaken during the 1980s under the sponsorship of Educational Testing Service, the College Board, and the Graduate Record Examinations Board (Willingham et al., 1988; see Zwick, 2002, pp. 99-100). The research program focused on issues involving candidates with disabilities who took the SAT or the (paper-and-pencil) GRE. The accuracy with which test scores could predict subsequent grades for students who tested with and without accommodations was investigated. The researchers concluded that in most cases the scores of test-takers who received accommodations were roughly comparable to scores obtained by nondisabled test-takers under standard conditions.

The one major exception to this conclusion involved test-takers who were granted extended time. These students had typically been given up to 12 hours to complete the SAT and up to 6 hours for the GRE, compared with about 3 hours for the standard versions of these tests. In general, the students who received extended time were more likely to finish the test than were candidates at standard test administrations, but this finding in itself did not lead to the conclusion that time limits for students with disabilities were too liberal in general. For SAT-takers claiming to have learning disabilities, however, the researchers found that "the data most clearly suggested that providing longer amounts of time may raise scores beyond the level appropriate to compensate for the disability" (Willingham et al., 1988, p. 156). In particular, these students' subsequent college grades were lower than their test scores predicted, and the greater the extended time, the greater the discrepancy. By contrast, the college performance of these students was consistent with their high school grades, suggesting that their SAT scores were inflated by excessively liberal time limits. Similar conclusions have been obtained in more recent SAT analyses (Cahalan et al., 2002), as well as studies of ACT and LSAT results for candidates with learning disabilities (Wightman, 1993; Ziomek and Andrews, 1996).

Another study that made use of external data was an investigation by Weston (2002) of the validity of scores from an "oral accommodation" on a fourth grade math test based on the National Assessment of Educational Progress (NAEP). The accommodation consisted of having the test read aloud to students. The sample included test-takers with and without disabilities. Each student took two matched forms of the test, one with the accommodation and one without. Weston collected external data in the form of teachers' ratings of the students on 33 mathematical operations and teachers' rankings of the students on overall math and reading ability. He hypothesized that "accommodated test scores will be more consonant with teachers' ratings of student ability than non-accommodated tests" (p. 4). Weston concluded that there was some slight support for his hypothesis.

While research that investigates relationships between assessment results and external criterion variables is valuable, it is important to note that in the context of K-12 assessment, there are few clearly useful criterion variables like the ones that can be compared with results from college entrances and certification tests. While teacher assessments and ratings, classroom grades, and other concurrent measures may be available, they are relatively unreliable. When weak relationships are found, it is difficult to know whether they indicate low levels of criterion validity or reflect the poor quality of the external criterion measures. Moreover, because prediction of future performance is not the purpose of NAEP or of state assessments, the evidence of validity of interpretations from these assessment results must be different in nature from that used for the SAT and similar tests. These issues are addressed in greater detail in Chapter 6.

VALIDITY RESEARCH PLANNED FOR NAEP

Staff of the National Center for Education Statistics provided the committee with an overview of studies currently in the planning stage that seek to answer questions about the validity of interpretations of results for accommodated administrations of NAEP. One of the planned studies involves examining the cognitive processes required for NAEP items through the use of a "think aloud" approach. NAEP-like items would be administered to small groups of students with disabilities and English language learners in a cognitive lab setting. Testing conditions would be systematically manipulated to study the effects of specific accommodations. This study is expected to provide information about the nature of the construct when students are assessed under accommodated and unaccommodated conditions.

A second study will examine the effects of providing extended time for responding to NAEP-like assessment items in reading and mathematics. Students with and without disabilities will be asked to respond to both multiple-choice and constructed response items under standard and extended timing conditions. An alternate performance measure will also be administered to allow for investigation of criterion validity (this is an example of a criterion variable that is relatively reliable for the K-12 context).

A third study will focus on the effects of providing calculators as an accommodation. Currently NAEP does not permit the use of calculators in the portions of the mathematics assessments that evaluate computational skills. As part of this study, students with and without disabilities will take the mathematics assessment with and without the accommodation. Performance on both kinds of items (those assessing computation and those not assessing computation) will be compared for both kinds of accommodations and both disability conditions. Data on an external criterion of mathematics skills (e.g., grades in mathematics courses) will also be collected so that criterion validity can be investigated.

SUMMARY AND RECOMMENDATIONS FOR
FUTURE VALIDITY RESEARCH

Determining whether accommodated scores are more valid representations of students' capabilities than unaccommodated ones requires that external data on the students' capabilities be obtained. Some possible external measures or criteria are teacher ratings, self-ratings, grade-point averages, course grades, and scores on alternative tests such as state tests. Analyses can then be conducted to determine whether the association between the test score of interest and the criterion variables is the same for accommodated and unaccommodated versions of the test. A conclusion that the association is indeed the same supports the validity of inferences made from accommodated scores.

Like all validity research, this type of analysis is more complicated in practice than in principle. First, the identification of an appropriate criterion measure may not be straightforward. Because college admissions tests are intended to predict college grades, the criterion variable for the Cahalan et al. (2002) study was relatively clear-cut, but this will not be true in the majority of cases. Moreover, as has been noted, suitable criterion variables are much less readily available in the K-12 context than in college admissions testing and other contexts, and those that are readily available are not very reliable. Second, it may be difficult to obtain data on the criterion once it is identified. That is, it is difficult to obtain external data that might be useful, such as teacher ratings or grades. Moreover, asking tested students to take a second assessment in order to provide a criterion measure is difficult in an environment in which most children are already spending significant amounts of their time being tested for various purposes. Obtaining external data is especially difficult for NAEP, in which individual participants are not ordinarily identified.

Third, except in an experimental setting like those in Weston (2002) and the criterion validity studies proposed for NAEP, the determination of whether the test-criterion relationships are the same for accommodated and unaccommodated administrations is complicated by the confounding of disability or English language learner status and accommodation status. That is, in a natural setting, those who use accommodations are likely to be students with disabilities or English language learners, and they are likely to differ from other students on many dimensions. Sireci et al. (2003, p. 25) allude to one aspect of this point in their remarks on the Cahalan et al. (2002) study: Sireci et al. point out that students with and without disabilities are likely to differ in course-taking patterns, and that this disparity should be taken into account when comparing the degree to which accommodated and unaccommodated SAT scores predict college grade-point average. Moreover, the differences among students with disabilities and English language learners in course-taking, general courses of study, teacher assignments, the instructional methods they are likely to experience, and the like, all compound the difficulty of obtaining usable criterion variables.

A final limitation of this type of validity assessment is that the accuracy of the criterion measure may differ across student groups, making it difficult to determine whether the test-criterion relationships are the same. For example, Willingham et al. (1988) and Cahalan et al. (2002) found that the correlations between admissions test scores and subsequent grade-point averages were smaller for candidates with disabilities. Willingham et al. found that the correlations between previous grades and subsequent grades were also smaller for students with disabilities. They speculated that one reason that grades were predicted more poorly for students with disabilities may be the exceptionally wide range in the quality of educational programs and grading standards for these students. These individuals may also be more likely than other students to experience difficulties in college or graduate school that affect their academic performance, such as inadequate support services or insufficient funds to support their studies.

A considerable amount of research into the effects of accommodations on test performance for students with disabilities and English language learners has been conducted to date. However, this research fails to provide a systematic, comprehensive investigation into the central issue of the validity of interpretations of scores from accommodated versions of assessments. Numerous reviews of the research into the effects of accommodations on test performance assessments (e.g., Chiu and Pearson, 1999; Tindal and Fuchs, 2000; Thompson et al., 2002; Sireci et al., 2003) make clear that the findings from existing research are inclusive and insufficient for test developers and users of test data to make informed decisions about either the appropriateness of different accommodations or the validity of inferences based on scores from accommodated administrations of assessments. The problems are twofold. First, taken as a whole, the body of research suggests contradictory findings, and solid conclusions cannot be drawn from it. For example, Thompson et al. (2002, p. 11) reviewed seven studies in which extended time was the accommodation. In four of these, extended time had a "positive effect on scores"; in three extended time had "no significant effect on scores." Similarly, in nine studies they reviewed on the effects of allowing computer administration, four showed "positive effects on scores," three showed "no significant effects," and two showed that it "altered item comparability." Diverse results such as these illustrate the difficulties facing policy makers who want to rely on the research in developing policy.

Second, in our view, research that examines the effects of accommodations in terms of gains or losses associated with taking the test with or without accommodations is not a means of evaluating the validity of inferences based on accommodated scores. Such research does not provide evidence that scores for students who take a test under standard conditions are comparable to scores for students who take a test under accommodated conditions or that similar interpretations can be based on results obtained under different conditions.

Thus the committee concludes that:

CONCLUSION 5-1: Most of the existing research demonstrates that accommodations do affect test scores but that the nature of the effects varies by individual.

CONCLUSION 5-2: For the most part, existing research has investigated the effects of accommodations on test performance but is not informative about the validity of inferences based on scores from accommodated administrations. That is, existing research does not provide information about the extent to which inferences based on scores obtained from accommodated administrations are comparable to inferences based on scores obtained from unaccommodated administrations. Furthermore, the research does not provide definitive evidence about which accommodations would produce the most valid estimates of performance.

Based on these findings, the committee believes that a program of research is needed that would systematically investigate the extent to which scores obtained from accommodated and unaccommodated test administrations are comparable and support similar kinds of inferences about the performance of students with disabilities and English language learners on NAEP and other large-scale assessments.

RECOMMENDATION 5-1: Research should be conducted that focuses on the validation of inferences based on accommodated assessments of students with disabilities and English language learners. Further research should be guided by a conceptual argument about the way accommodations are intended to function and the inferences the test results are intended to support. This research should include a variety of approaches and types of evidence, such as analyses of test content, test-takers' cognitive processes, and criterion-related evidence, and other studies deemed appropriate.

CONCLUSION

Available research has not adequately investigated the extent to which different accommodations for students with disabilities and English language learners may affect the validity of inferences based on scores from NAEP and other large-scale assessments. While research has shed some light on the ways accommodations function and on some aspects of their effects on test performance, in the committee's view, a central component of validity has been missing from much of this research. Without a well articulated validation argument that explicitly specifies the claims and intended inferences that underlie NAEP and other assessments, and that also explicitly specifies possible counterclaims and competing inferences, research into the effects of accommodations on assessments of students with disabilities and English language learners is likely to consist largely of a series of loosely connected studies that investigate various accommodations, more or less at random. An approach and a framework for articulating a logical validation argument for an assessment is discussed in the next chapter.

6

Articulating Validation Arguments

Accommodations are necessary to enable many students with disabilities and English language learners to participate in NAEP and other large-scale assessments. Because there is no definitive science to guide decisions about when an accommodation is needed or what kind is needed, there is always a risk that an accommodation will overcorrect or undercorrect in a way that further distorts a student's performance and undermines validity. For this reason, it cannot simply be assumed that scores from standard and accommodated administrations are comparable.

Decisions about accommodations are often made on the basis of common-sense judgments about the nature of the disability or linguistic difficulty and about the concepts and skills to be evaluated on the assessment. These decisions are often made on the basis of beliefs that may not be supported by empirical evidence, either because the type of empirical evidence needed is not available or because available research is not consulted. This is the case both for determining which accommodations are right for individuals and for developing policy about allowable and nonallowable accommodations.

To investigate the extent to which accommodations for students with disabilities and English language learners may affect the validity of inferences based on scores from NAEP and other assessments, one must begin with a close look at the validation arguments that underpin these scores in general. Research can most effectively investigate the effects of accommodations if it is based on a well articulated validation argument that explicitly specifies the claims underlying the assessments and the inferences the assessments are designed to support, and also if it explicitly specifies possible counterclaims and competing inferences.

The research conducted in this area to date has, for the most part, been inconclusive (Sireci et al., 2003). This is not to say that the existing research is not useful. Indeed, many of the studies of accommodations on NAEP and other large-scale assessments have been well designed and implemented. However, as described in Chapter 5, they have for the most part focused on differences in scores for students taking tests with and without various accommodations. They have not investigated the comparability of scores obtained from accommodated and unaccommodated administrations, nor have they illuminated the extent to which similar inferences can be drawn about scores obtained under different conditions. In our view, research should more specifically address the central validity concerns that have been raised about the inferences that can be drawn from scores based on accommodated administrations, and this process should begin with articulation of the validation argument that underlies performance on the assessment.

One purpose that can be served by this report, therefore, is to suggest an alternative approach to research on the validity of scores from accommodated administrations. We do this by suggesting ways in which an inference-based validation argument for NAEP could be articulated. Such an argument would provide a basis for conducting validation research that systematically investigates the effects of different accommodations on the performance of students with disabilities and English language learners. Such a validation argument would also inform assessment design and development, since the effects of different alterations in task characteristics and in test administration conditions caused by accommodations could be better understood using this approach.

In this chapter we lay out a procedure for making a systematic logical argument about:

- the skills and knowledge an assessment is intended to evaluate (target skills),
- the additional skills and knowledge an individual needs to demonstrate his or her proficiency with the target skills (ancillary skills), and
- the accommodations that would be appropriate, given the particular target and ancillary skills called for in a given assessment and the particular disability or language development profile that characterizes a given test-taker.

We begin with an analysis of the target and ancillary skills required to respond to NAEP reading and mathematics items. We then discuss procedures for articulating the validation argument using an approach referred to as evidence-centered design investigated by Mislevy and his colleagues (Hansen and Steinberg, 2004; Hansen et al., 2003; Mislevy et al., 2002, 2003). We illustrate the application of this approach with a sample NAEP fourth grade reading task. This example demonstrates how the suitability of various accommodations for students with disabilities and English language learners in NAEP can be evaluated, based on an articulation of the target skills being measured and the content of the assessment tasks in a particular assessment.

TARGET AND ANCILLARY SKILLS REQUIRED BY NAEP READING AND MATHEMATICS ITEMS

The committee commissioned a review of NAEP's reading and math frameworks with two goals in mind. First, we wanted to identify the constructs—targeted skills and knowledge—measured by the assessments and the associated ancillary skills required to perform the assessment tasks (see Hansen and Steinberg, 2004). We also wanted to evaluate the validation argument associated with use of specific accommodations on these assessments and to examine possible sources of alternate interpretations of scores. The resulting paper develops Bayes nets ("belief networks" that represent the interrelationships among many variables) to represent the test developer's conceptions of target and ancillary skills and the role of specific accommodations. The authors analyzed these models to evaluate the validity of specific accommodations. The reader is referred to Hansen et al. (2003) for an in-depth treatment of this topic.

In the text that follows, we summarize the Hansen et al. analysis of the NAEP reading and mathematics frameworks. We then draw on the work of Hansen, Mislevy, and their colleagues (Hansen and Steinberg, 2004; Hansen et al., 2003; Mislevy et al., 2002, 2003) to provide a very basic introduction to the development of an inference-based validation argument. We then discuss two examples, one adapted from Hansen and Steinberg (2004); see also Hansen et al., (2003) (a visually impaired student taking the NAEP reading assessment) and one that the committee developed (an English language learner taking the NAEP reading assessment).

According to the framework document, the NAEP reading assessment "measures comprehension by asking students to read passages and answer questions about what they have read" (National Assessment Governing Board, 2002a, p. 5). NAEP reading tasks are designed to evaluate skills in three reading contexts: reading for literary experience, reading for information, and reading to perform a task (p. 8). The tasks and questions also evaluate students' skills in four aspects of reading: forming a general understanding, developing interpretations, making reader-text connections, and examining content and structure (p. 11). These skills are considered by reading researchers to be components of reading comprehension. We note here that there are no explicit statements in the NAEP reading framework document to indicate that the assessment designers believe that decoding or fluency are part of the targeted proficiency (Hansen and Steinberg, 2004).

The NAEP mathematics assessment measures knowledge of mathematical content in five areas: number properties and operations, measurement, geometry, data analysis and probability, and algebra (National Assessment Governing

Board, 2001, p. 8). A second dimension of the math items is level of complexity: low, moderate, and high. Low-complexity items require recall and recognition of previously learned concepts. Moderate-complexity items require students to "use reasoning and problem solving strategies to bring together skill and knowledge from various domains." Highly complex items require test-takers "to engage in reasoning, planning, analysis, judgment, and creative thought." Each level of complexity includes aspects of knowing and doing math, such as "reasoning, performing procedures, understanding concepts, or solving problems" (p. 9). According to the frameworks, at each grade level approximately two-thirds of the assessment measures mathematical knowledge and skills without allowing access to a calculator; the other third allows the use of a calculator. Thus, the target constructs for the NAEP mathematics assessment seem to be content knowledge, reasoning and problem solving skills (Hansen and Steinberg, 2004), and, for some items, computational skills. Although content vocabulary (math vocabulary) is not specifically described as a skill being assessed, it seems to be an important aspect of the construct (Hansen and Steinberg, 2004).

Given the description of NAEP tasks in the mathematics and reading frameworks, Hansen and Steinberg (2004) identified several key ancillary skills that are required to respond to NAEP items, as shown in Tables 6-1 and 6-2. These

TABLE 6-1 Target and Ancillary Skills Required to Respond to Items on NAEP's Reading Assessment

Knowledge and/or Skill	Classification
Comprehend written text	Target skill
Know vocabulary	Ancillary skill
Decode text	Not specified as target skill
Reading fluency	Not specified as target skill
See the item	Ancillary skill
Hear the directions	Ancillary skill

TABLE 6-2 Target and Ancillary Skills Required to Respond to Items on NAEP's Mathematics Assessment

Knowledge and/or Skill	Classification
Mathematical reasoning	Target skill
Know content vocabulary	Target skill
Perform computations	Target skill
Comprehend written text	Ancillary skill
Know noncontent vocabulary	Ancillary skill
See the item	Ancillary skill
Hear the instructions	Ancillary skill

tables show a posible set of target and ancillary skills for the reading and mathematics assessments, respectively.

NATURE OF A VALIDATION ARGUMENT
AND THE VALIDATION PROCESS

Students' performance on assessment tasks is understood to accurately reflect the degree of their knowledge or skills in the area targeted. That is, if a test-taker's response to an assessment task is correct or receives a high rating, one infers that he or she possesses a high degree of the relevant target skills or knowledge; one infers a correspondingly low degree if his or her response is incorrect or receives a low rating. For all test-takers, there are likely to be some possible alternative explanations for test performance. In a reading assessment task, for example, it may be possible for a test-taker to answer some of the tasks correctly simply by guessing or as a consequence of prior familiarity with the reading passage or its subject matter, despite poor reading skills. In this case, these potential alternative explanations for good performance weaken the claim or inference about the test-taker's reading ability.

Alternative explanations can also potentially account for poor performance; for instance, if a test-taker is not feeling well on the day of the assessment and does not perform as well as he or she could, the results would not reflect his or her reading ability. Of most concern in this context are deficiencies in the specific ancillary skills required to respond to an item that may interfere with the measurement of the targeted constructs.

Validation is essentially the process of building a case in support of a particular interpretation of test scores (Kane, 1992; Kane et al., 1999; Messick, 1989, 1994). According to Bachman (in press, p. 267) the validation process includes two interrelated activities:

- articulating an argument that provides the logical framework for linking test performance to an intended interpretation and use and
- collecting relevant evidence in support of the intended interpretations and uses.

In their work on evidence-centered test design, Mislevy and his colleagues (Hansen and Steinberg, 2004; Hansen et al., 2003; Mislevy et al., 2003) expand on this notion, using Toulmin's approach to the structure of arguments to describe an interpretive argument (Mislevy et al., 2003, p. 11; and Hansen and Steinbeg, 2004, p. 17) and use the following terminology to describe the argument:

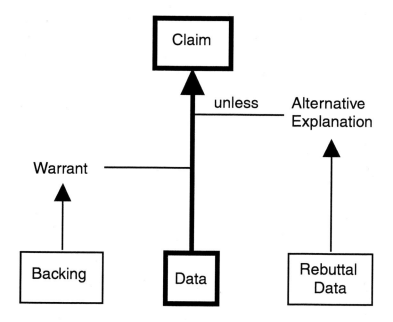

FIGURE 6-1 Toulmin diagram of the structure of arguments.
SOURCE: Adapted from Hansen et al. (2003).

- A *claim* is the inference that test designers want to make, on the basis of the observed data, about what test-takers know or can do. (Claims specify the target skills and knowledge.)
- The *data* are the responses of test-takers to assessment tasks, that is, what they say or do.
- A *warrant* is a general proposition used to justify the inference from the data to the claim.
- A warrant is based on *backing*, which is derived from theory, research, or experience.
- *Alternative explanations* are rival hypotheses that might account for the observed performance on an assessment task. (Alternative explanations are often related to ancillary skills and knowledge.)
- *Rebuttal data* provide further details on the possible alternate explanations for score variation, and can either support or weaken the alternative explanations.

The structure of this argument is illustrated in Figure 6-1, in which the arrow from the data to the claim represents an inference that is justified on the basis of a warrant.

Illustrative Examples

To illustrate the articulation of a validation argument for NAEP, we use a released NAEP fourth grade reading assessment task called "A Brick to Cuddle Up To," which is described as an informational text (National Assessment Governing Board, 2002a) (see Box 6-1). We use this task to illustrate our notion of how a validation argument can make it easier to identify target and ancillary skills, as well as appropriate accommodations for students with disabilities and English language learners.

Example 1:
Sue, a Visually Impaired Student Taking a NAEP Reading Assessment

A validity argument in support of inferences to be made on the basis of scores for the "Brick to Cuddle Up To" reading tasks might look like the following:

Backing: [According to] cognitive research, reading is purposeful and active. According to this view, a reader reads a text to understand what is read, construct memory representations of what is understood, and put this understanding to use (p. 5).

Warrant: When reading an informational text, Proficient-level fourth graders should be able to draw reasonable conclusions from the text, recognize relationships such as cause and effect or similarities and differences . . . . Basic-level fourth graders should be able to . . . connect ideas from the text to their background knowledge and experiences (p. 28).

Suppose that Sue responds incorrectly to NAEP reading items.

Data: Sue responded incorrectly to tasks that required her to connect ideas from the text to her background knowledge and experience and that required her to draw reasonable conclusions from the text and to recognize relationships such as cause and effect or similarities and differences.

Claim: Sue is a below Basic-level fourth grade reader.[1]

This argument is illustrated in Figure 6-2.

Validation Argument for Performance on NAEP Fourth Grade Reading Assessment Task. There are a number of possible alternative explanations for

---

[1]This example is designed only to illustrate the principle; no such claim would actually be made on the basis of only a single test item.

BOX 6-1
Sample NAEP Item Entitled "A Brick to Cuddle Up To"

Imagine shivering on a cold winter's night. The tip of your nose tingles in the frosty air. Finally, you climb into bed and find the toasty treat you have been waiting for—your very own hot brick.

If you had lived in colonial days, that would not sound as strange as it does today. Winters were hard in this New World, and the colonists had to think of clever ways to fight the cold. At bedtime, they heated soapstones, or bricks, in the fireplaces. They wrapped the bricks in cloths and tucked them into their beds. The brick kept them warm at night, at least for as long as its heat lasted.

Before the colonists slipped into bed, they rubbed their icy sheets with a bed warmer. This was a metal pan with a long wooden handle. The pan held hot embers from the fireplace. It warmed the bedding so well that sleepy bodies had to wait until the sheets cooled before climbing in.

Staying warm wasn't just a bedtime problem. On winter rides, colonial travelers covered themselves with animal skins and warm blankets. Tucked under the blankets, near their feet, were small tin boxes called foot stoves. A foot stove held burning coals. Hot smoke puffed from small holes in the stove's lid, soothing freezing feet and legs. When the colonists went to Sunday services, their foot stoves, furs, and blankets went with them. The meeting houses had no heat of their own until the 1800s.

At home, colonial families huddled close to the fireplace, or hearth. The fireplace was wide and high enough to hold a large fire, but its chimney was large, too. That caused a problem: Gusts of cold air blew into the house. The area near the fire was warm, but in the rest of the room it might still be cold enough to see your breath.

Reading or needlework was done by candlelight or by the light of the fire. During the winter, animal skins sealed the drafty windows of some cabins and blocked out the daylight. The living area inside was gloomy, except in the circle of light at the hearth.

Early Americans did not bathe as often as we do. When they did, their "bathroom" was the kitchen, in that toasty space by the hearth. They partially filled a tub of cold water, then warmed it up with water heated in the fireplace. A blanket draped from chairs for privacy also let the fire's warmth surround the bather.

The household cooks spent hours at the hearth. They stirred the kettle of corn pudding or checked the baking bread while the rest of the family carried on their own fireside activities. So you can see why the fireplace was the center of a colonial home. The only time the fire was allowed to die down was at bedtime. Ashes would be piled over the fire, reducing it to embers that might glow until morning.

By sunrise, the hot brick had become a cold stone once more. An early riser might get dressed under the covers, then hurry to the hearth to warm up.

Maybe you'd enjoy hearing someone who kept warm in these ways tell you what it was like. You wouldn't need to look for someone who has been living for two hundred years. In many parts of the country, the modern ways didn't take over from the old ones until recently. Your own grandparents or other older people might remember the warmth of a hearthside and the joy of having a brick to cuddle up to.

SOURCE: Used by permission of Highlights for Children, Inc., Columbus, OH. Copyright © 1991. Illustrations by Katherine Dodge.

Questions for "A Brick to Cuddle Up To"

1. **You would probably read this article if you wanted to know how the colonists**
   a. cooked their food
   b. traveled in the winter
   c. washed their clothes
   d. kept warm in cold weather
   [Aspect: General Understanding   Key: D   Percent correct: 85%]
2. **After reading this article, would you like to have lived during colonial times? What information in the article makes you think this?**
   (Responses to this question were scored according to a three-level rubric.)
   [Aspect: Reader/Text Connections   Percent Full Comprehension: 20%]
3. **Some of the ways that colonists kept warm during the winter were different from the ways that people keep warm today. Tell about two of these differences.**
   (Responses to this question were scored according to a three-level rubric.)
   [Aspect: Reader/Text Connections   Percent Full Comprehension: 17%]
4. **Do you think "A Brick to Cuddle Up To" is a good title for this article? Using information from the article, tell why or why not.**
   (Responses to this question were scored according to a three-level rubric.)
   [Aspect: Developing Interpretation   Percent Full Comprehension: 37%]
5. **Give two reasons stated in the article why the hearth was the center of the home in colonial times.**
   (Responses to this question were scored according to a three-level rubric.)
   [Aspect: Developing Interpretation   Percent Full Comprehension: 20%]
6. **A colonist would probably have used a foot stove when**
   a. going on a trip
   b. sleeping in bed
   c. sitting by the fireplace
   d. working around the house
   [Aspect: Developing Interpretation   Key: A   Percent correct: 36%]
7. **Pretend that you are an early American colonist. Describe at least three activities you might do during a cold winter evening. Be specific. Use details from the article to help you write your description.**
   (Responses to this question were scored according to a four-level rubric.)
   [Aspect: Developing Interpretation   Percent Extensive: 12%]
8. **In writing this article, the author mostly made use of**
   a. broad ideas
   b. specific details
   c. important questions
   d. interesting characters
   [Aspect: Examining Content and Structure   Key: B   Percent correct: 66%]
9. **Does the author help you understand what colonial life was like? Use examples from the article to explain why or why not.**
   (Responses to this question were scored according to a three-level rubric.)
   [Aspect: Examining Content and Structure   Percent Full Comprehension: 20%]

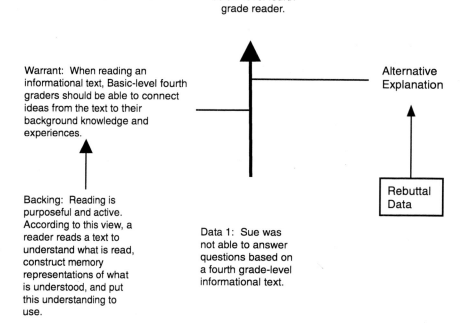

FIGURE 6-2 Validation argument for performance on NAEP fourth grade reading assessment task.

Sue's poor performance. For example, her decoding skill or reading fluency might be weak, which could interfere with her comprehension of the text. Alternatively, it might be that although she is visually impaired, Sue took a regular-sized font version of the test. If we know that Sue is visually impaired, then this constitutes rebuttal data that supports this alternative explanation (Figure 6-3).

Visual Impairment: Alternative Explanation for Performance on NAEP Fourth Grade Reading Assessment Task. In this example, if it is known that Sue's low score is a consequence of lack of visual acuity and that sight is an ancillary skill for the reading assessment, providing Sue with a large-font version of the test would allow her better access to the testing materials and would weaken the alternative explanation of poor vision as a reason for her performance. Another accommodation sometimes considered as a compensation for poor vision is having the test read orally. It is difficult to determine whether this accommodation is appropriate for the NAEP reading assessment, given that the reading framework does not state whether or not decoding and fluency are part of the

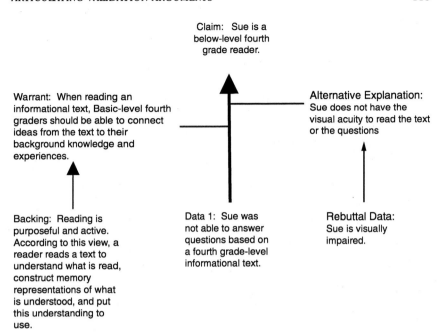

FIGURE 6-3 Alternative explanations for performance on NAEP fourth grade reading assessment task.

target construct. If the test were read aloud, Sue would not need to use her decoding and fluency skills in order to read the passage and respond to the questions. If decoding and fluency are considered to be an aspect of the target construct, then the read-aloud accommodation would alter that construct. If decoding and fluency are considered ancillary skills, then the read-aloud accommodation would simply provide Sue with easier access to the passage and questions so she could more accurately demonstrate her reading comprehension skills.

Example 2:
Tina, an English Language Learner Taking a NAEP Reading Assessment

A validity argument in support of inferences to be made on the basis of scores for the "Brick to Cuddle Up To" would work the same way for English language learners as for students with disabilities. In this example, however, the *data* are different. Suppose that Tina, an English language learner, were able to respond correctly to some of the tasks and not others. The data might be as follows:

Data: Tina read the passage, "A Brick to Cuddle Up To," which is a fourth grade-level informational text. Tina's written answer to the question, "After reading this article, would you like to have lived during colonial times? What information in the article makes you think this?" was scored as "Basic" on a three-level scoring rubric of "basic," "proficient" and "advanced." This question is intended to assess "Reader/Text Connections," and was a fairly difficult item, with only 20 percent of test-takers answering the question successfully (National Assessment Governing Board, 2002a, pp. 16-17.)

Claim: Tina is a Basic-level fourth grade reader.

This argument is illustrated in Figure 6-4. The figure highlights the fact that there are two sources of data in the argument. The first, labeled Data 1, consists of the test-taker's observed response to the assessment task, as described above. The second source, labeled Data 2, consists of the characteristics of the assessment tasks. Considering the characteristics of the task as part of the validation argument is critical for an investigation of the effects of accommodations for two reasons. First, accommodations can be viewed as changes to the characteristics or conditions of assessment tasks. Second, the test-taker's response is the result of an interaction between the test-taker and the task, and changing the characteristics or conditions of the task may critically alter this interaction in ways that affect the validity of the inferences that can be made on the basis of test performance. In the example above, some of the relevant characteristics of the task are:

1. the reading passage is developmentally appropriate for fourth graders,
2. the reading passage is classified as informational, and
3. the task requires the test-taker to connect ideas from the text to his or her background knowledge and experiences.

We have looked at the way in which an argument can support the claims or inferences an educational assessment was designed to support, but, as we have seen, there are a number of potential alternative explanations for any assessment results.[2] Variations in either the attributes of test-takers or the characteristics of assessment tasks can in some cases account for variations in performance that are unrelated to what is actually being measured—the variation among test-takers in what they actually know and can do. In such cases, the validity of the intended inferences is weakened. With students with disabilities and English language

---

[2]One set of alternative explanations, which consist of random variation and variation associated with particular aspects of the measurement procedure (e.g., items, raters, forms) have traditionally been dealt with under the rubric of reliability or dependability, rather than validity. In other words, these kinds of variation are explained by inconsistencies in administration, scoring, etc., rather than by differences in the nature of the task.

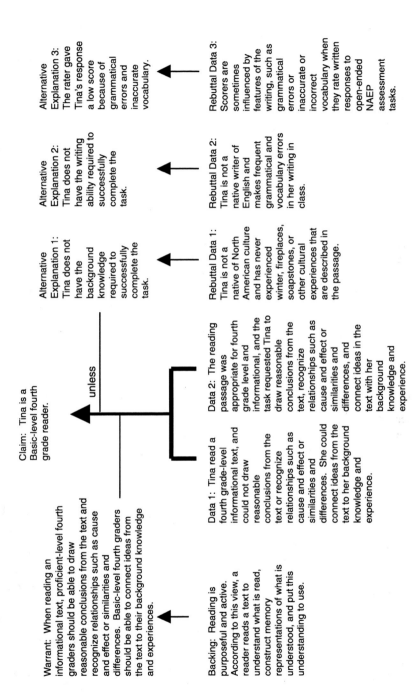

FIGURE 6-4 Alternative explanations for performance on NAEP fourth grade reading assessment task.

learners, test developers and administrators are presented with systematic variations in test-takers' attributes—they are systematic in that they are consistently
associated with these particular groups of test-takers. Hence, the attributes that
identify these groups may constitute alternative explanations for variations in
performance that are evident in scores, and thus these attributes may undermine
validity.

When the characteristics or conditions of the assessment tasks are altered, as
when test-takers are offered accommodations, another source of systematic variation is introduced. These alterations can yield results that are explained not by
differences in what students know and can do, but by the accommodations themselves. Moreover, when different groups of test-takers interact with different
kinds of accommodations, the results may vary and thus these interactions can
also constitute alternative explanations for performance. Therefore, in evaluating
the effects of accommodations on the validity of inferences, three kinds of alternative explanations need to be considered:

1. Performance may be affected systematically by attributes of individuals
   associated with specific groups, such as students with disabilities and
   English language learners.
2. Performance may be affected systematically by accommodations, changes
   in the characteristics, or conditions of assessment tasks.
3. Performance may be affected systematically by the interactions between
   the attributes of groups of test-takers and characteristics of assessment
   tasks.

One crucial distinction that psychometricians make is between construct-
relevant and construct-irrelevant variance in test scores, that is, variance that is or
is not related to the test-takers' status with respect to the construct being assessed
(Messick, 1989). All three of these alternative explanations could be viewed as
potential sources of construct-irrelevant variance in test performance.

The case that an alternative explanation accounts for score variation would
need to be based on rebuttal data that provides further details on the probable
reasons for score variation. Seen in the context of a validation argument, the
primary purpose of an assessment accommodation is to produce test results for
which the possible alternative explanations, such as test-taker characteristics that
are irrelevant to what is being measured, are weakened, while the intended inferences are not weakened.

The fourth grade NAEP reading task discussed earlier can be used to
demonstrate how one or more alternative explanations might work and the nature
of the rebuttal data that might support them. Suppose Tina is an English language
learner whose family's cultural heritage is not North American and who is not
familiar with some of the concepts presented in the passage, such as winter,
fireplaces, and soapstones. In this case, it could be that Tina's lack of familiarity

with some of the cultural elements of the passage, rather than inadequate reading proficiency, constitutes an alternative explanation for her performance; if this is true, it weakens the intended inference. It may well be that Tina's reading is better than the basic level described for fourth grade but that her lack of familiarity with important concepts prevented her from being able to answer the questions based on this passage correctly. The components of this argument are illustrated in Figure 6-5.

Exploring and generating alternative explanations for performance can be done only in the context of clear statements about the content and skills the task is intended to assess. To demonstrate how this type of information can be used in developing a validation argument, the same example can be tied to NAEP's documentation of the content and skills targeted by its fourth grade reading assessment. The NAEP Reading Framework explicitly recognizes that background knowledge is a factor in test performance but describes this factor as one that contributes to item difficulty. The framework document notes that "Item difficulty is a function of . . . the amount of background knowledge required to respond correctly" (National Assessment Governing Board, 2002a, p. 21). This statement leaves unanswered the question of whether or not background knowledge is crucial to the claim, or intended inference; in other words it does not specify whether background knowledge is a part of what is being assessed.

If the test-taker's degree of background knowledge is not part of the construct or claim, then it constitutes a potential source of construct-irrelevant variance. Furthermore, since item difficulty is essentially an artifact of the interaction between a test-taker and an assessment task (Bachman, 2002b), it would seem that the critical source of score variance that needs to be investigated in this case is not the task characteristic—the content of the reading passage—but rather the interaction between the test-taker's background knowledge and that content.

A second alternative explanation for Tina's performance in the example can be found in the nature of the expected response, and how this was scored. Consider an example: "After reading this article, would you like to have lived during colonial times? What information in the article makes you think this? (National Assessment Governing Board, 2002a, p. 41).

This question is intended to assess "reader/text connections," and test-takers are expected to respond with a "short constructed response" (National Center for Education Statistics, 2003a). This particular question is scored using a rubric[3] that defines three levels: "evidence of complete comprehension," "evidence of surface or partial comprehension," and "evidence of little or no comprehension" (National Assessment Governing Board, 2002a, p. 41). Tina's answer was scored as showing "evidence of little or no comprehension." The descriptor for this score level is as follows (National Assessment Governing Board, 2002a, p. 41):

---

[3]A rubric is a guide for scoring constructed response items. Constructed response items are those in which the test-taker supplies the response, rather than selecting it from a set of choices.

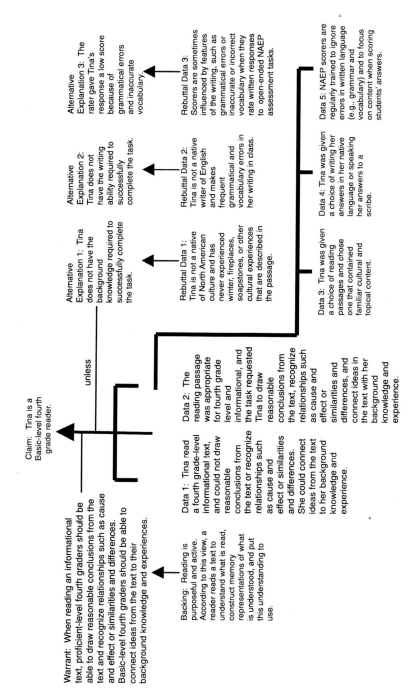

FIGURE 6-5 Accommodations to weaken alternative explanations for performance on NAEP.

These responses contain inappropriate information from the article or personal opinions about the article but do not demonstrate an understanding of what it was like to live during colonial times as described in the article. They may answer the question, but provide no substantive explanation.

The fact that this question requires students to write a response in English provides a second alternative explanation; specifically, that Tina's first language is not English, and her writing skills in English are poor. This also points to a third alternative explanation, that the individual who scored Tina's answer gave her a low score because of the poor quality of her writing. This potential problem with the scoring of English language learners' written responses to academic achievement test tasks is discussed in National Research Council (1997b), which points out that "errors . . . result from inaccurate and inconsistent scoring of open-ended performance-based measures. There is evidence the scorers may pay attention to linguistic features of performance unrelated to the content of the assessment" (p. 122). These additional alternative explanations and the rebuttal evidence are also presented in Figure 6-5.

To understand what constitutes an inappropriate or invalid accommodation, as well as to describe current accommodations or to design new accommodations that may be more appropriate for different groups of test-takers, a framework for systematically describing the characteristics of assessment tasks is needed. Bachman and Palmer (1996) present a framework of task characteristics that may be useful in describing the ways in which the characteristics and conditions of assessment tasks are altered for the purpose of accommodating students with disabilities and English language learners. This framework includes characteristics of the setting, the rubric, the input, and the expected response, as well as the relationships between input and response.

Bachman and Palmer maintain that these characteristics can be used to describe existing assessment tasks as well as to provide a basis for designing new types of assessment tasks. By changing the specific characteristics of a particular task, test developers can create an entirely new task. Accommodations that are commonly provided for students with disabilities or English language learners can also be described in terms of alterations in task characteristics, as in Table 6-3.

Task characteristics can be altered in such a way that the plausibility of alternative explanations for test results is lessened. This can be illustrated with the example used earlier, in which there were three possible alternative explanations for Tina's poor performance on the reading assessment. To weaken the first alternative explanation, that Tina's poor performance is the result of her lack of familiarity with the cultural content of the reading passage, test developers would need to control a characteristic of the input—in this case the content of the texts used in the assessment—to ensure that the texts presented to test-takers are not so unfamiliar as to interfere with their success on the assessment. One way to achieve this is to include students with disabilities and English language learners in the

TABLE 6-3 Task Characteristics Altered by Various Accommodations

Accommodation	Task Characteristics Altered
Individual and small-group administrations*	Setting—participants
Multiple sessions*	Setting—time of assessment
Special lighting*	Setting—physical characteristics
Extended time*	Rubric—time allotment
Oral reading of instructions*	Setting—participants
	Input—channel and vehicle of language of input
Large print*	Input—graphology
Bilingual version of test*	Input—language of input (Spanish vs. English)
Oral reading in English*	Setting—participants
	Input—channel of input (oral L1 vs. written L1)
Oral reading in native language*	Setting—participants
	Input—language and channel of input (oral L1 vs. written L2)
Braille writers*	Setting—physical characteristics-equipment
	Expected response—channel of response
Answer orally*	Expected response—channel of response
Scribe*	Setting—participants
	Expected response—channel of response
Tape recorders	Setting—physical characteristics-equipment, equipment
	Expected response—channel of response (oral vs. written)

*Accommodation provided in NAEP.

pretesting of items, and possibly to pretest items using cognitive labs. Nevertheless, even with a very large bank of pretested texts, there will still be some probability that a particular test-taker will be unfamiliar with a given text, and this interaction effect will be very difficult to eliminate entirely.

To weaken the second alternative explanation, that Tina's poor performance on reading assessment is the result of poor writing skills (which are not being assessed), either or both of two characteristics of the expected response—language or mode of response—could be altered. If Tina can read and write reasonably well in her native language, she might be permitted to write her responses in her native language. If she cannot write well in her native language but is reasonably fluent orally in English, then she could be permitted to speak her answers to a scribe, who would write them for her. If she is also not fluent orally in English, then she could be permitted to speak her answers in her native language to a scribe. The appropriateness of these alterations of course depends on the targeted construct. These alterations in task characteristics are shown in Table 6-4. These different accommodations provide data that weaken the possible alternative arguments and thus strengthen the inferences that were intended to be made based on Tina's scores.

TABLE 6-4 Alterations in Task Characteristics as a Consequence of Accommodations

Task Characteristic	Unaccommodated Task	Accommodated Task 1	Accommodated Task 2	Accommodated Task 3
Language of response	English	Native language	English	Native language
Channel of response	Visual: Writing	Visual: Writing	Oral: Speaking	Oral: Speaking

To weaken the third alternative explanation, that Tina's poor reading performance is the result of the scorer's using the wrong scoring criteria, the test developers need to control two characteristics of the scoring process: the criteria used for scoring and the scorers themselves. Such corrections are handled most effectively through rigorous and repeated scorer training sessions.

Figure 6-5 portrays the relationships between the alternative explanations, rebuttal data, and types of data needed to weaken the alternative explanations.

SUMMARY AND CONCLUSIONS

In this chapter we have discussed the components of the kind of validation argument that underlies the intended inferences to be made from any assessment. We have illustrated how intended inferences, or claims, about test-takers' target skills or knowledge need to be based both on warrants that are backed by relevant theory or research findings, and on data. These data consist of two types: (1) the test-taker's response to the assessment task and (2) the characteristics of the assessment task. We have explained that a variety of test-takers' characteristics, such as disabilities, insufficient proficiency in English, or lack of cultural knowledge, can constitute alternative explanations for their performance on assessments. We have also discussed the ways specific accommodations can be described in terms of specific aspects of the assessment tasks and administration procedures.

The committee has reviewed a variety of materials about the NAEP assessment (National Assessment Governing Board [NAGB], 2001, 2002a, 2002b; National Center for Education Statistics, 2003a, 2003b) and has heard presentations by NAEP and NAGB officials about these topics. In light of the validity issues related to inclusion and accommodations for students with disabilities and English language learners that have been discussed, we draw the following conclusions:

CONCLUSION 6-1: The validation argument for NAEP is not as well articulated as it should be with respect to inferences based on accommodated versions of NAEP assessments.

CONCLUSION 6-2: Even when the validation argument is well articulated, there is insufficient evidence to support the validity of inferences based on alterations in NAEP assessment tasks or administrative procedures for accommodating students with disabilities and English language learners.

On the basis of these conclusions we make three recommendations to NAEP officials. Although these recommendations are specific to NAEP, we strongly urge the sponsors of other large-scale assessment programs to consider them as well.

RECOMMENDATION 6-1: NAEP officials should identify the inferences that they intend should be made from its assessment results and clearly articulate the validation arguments in support of those inferences.

RECOMMENDATION 6-2: NAEP officials should embark on a research agenda that is guided by the claims and counterclaims for intended uses of results in the validation argument they have articulated. This research should apply a variety of approaches and types of evidence, such as analyses of test content, test-takers' cognitive processes, criterion-related evidence, and other studies deemed appropriate.

RECOMMENDATION 6-3: NAEP officials should conduct empirical research to specifically evaluate the extent to which the validation argument that underlies each NAEP assessment and the inferences the assessment was designed to support are affected by the use of particular accommodations.

7

Implications of the Committee's Conclusions and Recommendations

IMPLICATIONS FOR NAEP

The work of this committee was stimulated by concerns about including students with disabilities and English language learners in the National Assessment of Educational Progress (NAEP) and about the effects that accommodations they receive may have on their performance. The National Center for Education Statistics, which initiated the study, asked the NRC to examine NAEP's policies regarding the inclusion of students with disabilities and English language learners in its assessments, the use of accommodations for these students, and a variety of questions related to these issues. In response, the committee has focused much of its attention on reasons why NAEP officials should review their policies in both of these areas, compare them with those of the states, and work toward greater consistency between NAEP's policies and those used in the states.

We have recommended that NAEP continue to pursue the goal of maximizing the participation of all students, and that NAEP officials be mindful of the requirements states must meet under the No Child Left Behind Act, recognizing that even though no formal comparisons of state scores to NAEP results are required, NAEP is frequently viewed as an informal benchmark for state results. We hope that this report makes evident that the committee believes it is very important that the sometimes stark differences between the policies in effect for NAEP and those used by states be recognized, and, to the extent possible, reduced.

At the same time, NAEP has in many ways been a model for the assessment community. Much groundbreaking research has been conducted by NAEP's sponsors and others associated with the NAEP program, such as Educational

Testing Service (ETS). The developers of NAEP assessments have taken advantage of advances in educational measurement and have been early users of new item types and modes of assessment, such as constructed-response formats, items that require the use of calculators, items that require students to interact with objects such as atlases or scientific specimens, and the like. The NAEP Arts assessment, for example, has demonstrated the willingness of NAEP's sponsors and assessment developers to explore new ways of gaining information about students' knowledge and skills. With examples such as these, NAEP has motivated many states to consider and adopt more creative testing approaches than they had been using (National Research Council, 2000a).

Given this record, the committee believes that NAEP has a responsibility to take the lead as well on the complex issues surrounding the assessment of students with disabilities and English language learners. NAEP has published one study on the validity of accommodations that uses an external criterion variable (Weston), and several other studies are underway. We encourage NAEP to continue to pursue research that follows this model. More generally, we hope that the recommendations in this report will spur NAEP's sponsors to set an example of forward-looking research and practice in these areas.

IMPLICATIONS FOR STATES

Although most of the committee's messages have been directed to those who develop policy for NAEP and who are responsible for its technical soundness, the issues raised in this report have important implications for state and local assessment programs as well. Points that are relevant to states have been mentioned in several places, and the committee has offered one specific recommendation to states (Recommendation 4-5). However, we close the report with a discussion of the broader implications of our findings and conclusions for states because it is the states that are struggling most immediately with the technical challenges of assessing students with disabilities and English language learners.

The No Child Left Behind legislation has been the source of considerable urgency for states' efforts to collect data about students' academic achievement. As we have noted in earlier chapters, the requirement for assessing students and managing the resulting data under this law is steep. Yet previous NRC committees and others have already documented evidence that the collection and reporting of assessment results for these two groups were insufficient even before the No Child Left Behind Act took effect (e.g., National Research Council, 1997a, 1997b, 1999a; Thurlow et al., 2002), and the need for such data does not arise solely because of that law.

With regard to students with disabilities, an NRC committee specifically noted that large-scale studies of education issues frequently fail to include these students in their samples or include them in ways that are not systematic (National Research Council, 1997a, pp. 209-210). That committee called for data on how students with disabilities compare with other students on many variables related to their schooling and educational achievement. They pointed out the need for research to investigate the relationship between accommodations and validity, not only to document the effects of various accommodations on test scores but also to develop criteria for deciding which accommodations will preserve the validity and usefulness of test results. This committee also noted the need for research to support the development of reliable and valid alternate assessments, and the equating and scaling of such alternatives.

There are even fewer data available for English language learners. For example, simply finding out how many fourth graders across the country are English language learners cannot readily be done with available data. National demographic data on limited English proficient students have been gathered for decades in the U.S. Department of Education's Survey of the States' Limited English Proficient Students and Available Education Programs and Services of Education. However, the quality of the data is uncertain because different states have used different criteria for the identification of students of limited English proficiency (summary reports available from National Clearinghouse on English Language Acquisition: http://www.ncela.gwu.edu). An NRC report on the schooling of language minority children identified specific research needs related to the assessment of these children (National Research Council, 1997b, pp. 128-131). It noted in particular the need for research that links assessment strategies to the knowledge base regarding language acquisition, and that can assist in the development of guidelines for when and how to assess these students, and for the development of accurate and consistent means of scoring the work of English language learners.

There is in general, as we have discussed, a lack of research findings that could be used to help policy makers, administrators, and others make decisions about when and how to offer accommodations to students with different kinds of needs. There is a particular need for research into the validity of interpretations made from accommodated scores, and we have described the direction we think this kind of research should take. We would encourage local education officials and schools to undertake such research, to take part in such research when it is conducted by others, and to provide data to researchers engaged in such research. We believe that such research is a crucial element in the effort to build an education system that strives to meet the needs of all students. In order that resources be adequately managed and that the needs of all students be recognized and addressed, those responsible for meeting these goals must have accurate information about all students.

References

Abedi, J. (2001a). *Assessment and accommodation for English language learners: Issues and recommendations.* (Policy Brief 4). Los Angeles, CA: National Center for Research on Evaluation, Standards, and Student Testing, University of California.

Abedi, J. (2001b). *Language accommodation for large-scale assessment in science: Assessing English language learners.* (Final Deliverable, Project 2.4 Accommodation). Los Angeles, CA: National Center for Research on Evaluation, Standards, and Student Testing, University of California.

Abedi, J., and Lord, C. (2001). The language factor in mathematics tests. *Applied Measurement in Education, 14* (3), 219-234.

Abedi, J., Lord, C., and Hofstetter, C. (1998). *Impact of selected background variables on students' NAEP math performance accommodations.* (CSE Tech. Rep. No. 478). Los Angeles, CA: Center for the Study of Evaluation, University of California.

Abedi, J., Lord, C. Boscardin, C., and Miyoshi, J. (2000). *The effects of accommodations on the assessment of LEP students in NAEP.* (CSE Tech. Rep. No 537). Los Angeles: National Center for Research on Evaluation, Standards, and Student Testing, University of California.

Abedi, J., Lord, C., Hofstetter, C., and Baker, E. (2000). Impact of accommodation strategies on English language learners' test performance. *Educational Measurement: Issues and Practice, 19*(3), 16-26.

Abedi, J., Courtney, M., Mirocha, J., Leon, S., and Goldberg, J. (2001). *Language accommodations for large-scale assessments in science.* Los Angeles, CA: National Center for Research on Evaluation, Standards, and Student Testing, University of California.

Abedi, J., Hofstetter, C., Baker, E., and Lord, C. (2001). *NAEP math performance and test accommodations: Interactions with student language background.* (CSE Tech. Rep. No. 536). Los Angeles, CA: National Center for Research on Evaluation, Standards, and Student Testing, University of California.

Albus, D., Bielinski, J., Thurlow, M., and Liu, K. (2001). *The effect of a simplified English language dictionary on a reading test* (LEP Projects Report 1). Minneapolis: University of Minnesota, National Center on Educational Outcomes.

126

American Educational Research Association, American Psychological Association, and National Council on Measurement in Education. (1999). *Standards for educational and psychological testing.* Washington, DC: Author.

Anderson, M., Liu, K., Swierzbin, B., Thurlow, M., and Bielinski, J. (2000). *Bilingual accommodations for limited English proficient students on statewide reading tests: Phase 2.* (Minnesota Report No. 31). Minneapolis, MN: University of Minnesota, National Center on Education Outcomes.

Bachman, L.F. (2002a). Alternative interpretations of alternative assessments: Some validity issues in educational performance assessments. *Educational Measurement: Issues and Practice, 21*(3), 5-18.

Bachman, L.F. (2002b). Some reflections on task-based language performance assessment. *Language Testing, 19*(4), 453-476.

Bachman, L.F. (in press). *Statistical analyses for language assessment.* Cambridge, MA: Cambridge University Press.

Bachman, L.F., and Palmer, A.S. (1996). *Language testing in practice: Designing and developing useful language tests.* Oxford, England: Oxford University Press.

Braun, H., Ragosta, M., and Kaplan, B. (1986). *The predictive validity of the Scholastic Aptitude Test for disabled students.* (Research Report 86-38). New York: College Entrance Examination Board.

Brown, P.J., and Augustine, A. (2001). *Screen reading software as an assessment accommodation: Implications for instruction and student performance.* Paper presented at the Annual Meeting of the American Educational Research Association, April 10-14, Seattle, WA.

Cahalan, C., Mandinach, E., and Camara, W. (2002). *Predictive validity of SAT I: Reasoning test for test takers with learning disabilities and extended time accommodations.* (College Board Research Report RR 2002-05). New York: College Board.

Camara, W., Copeland, T., and Rothchild, B. (1998). *Effects of extended time on the SAT I: Reasoning Test: Score growth for students with learning disabilities.* (College Board Research Report 98-7). New York: College Board.

Cardinet, J., Tournier, Y., and Allal, L. (1976). The symmetry of generalizability theory: Applications to educational measurement. *Journal of Educational Measurement, 13,* 119-135.

Castellon-Wellington, M. (1999). *The impact of preference for accommodations: The performance of English language learners on large-scale academic achievement tests.* (CSE Tech. Rep. No. 524). Los Angeles, CA: Center for the Study of Evaluation, Graduate School of Education and Information Studies, University of California.

Chiu, C.W.T., and Pearson, P.D. (1999). *Synthesizing the effects of test accommodations for special education and limited English proficient students.* Paper presented at the National Conference on Large Scale Assessment, June 13-16, Snowbird, UT.

Council of Chief State School Officers. (2002). *Annual survey of state student assessment programs 2000-2001: Summary report.* Washington DC: Author.

DeVito, P.J. (1996). *Issues relating to the future of National Assessment of Educational Progress: The state perspective.* Unpublished paper presented at the annual meeting of the American Educational Research Association, April.

Dunbar, S., Koretz, D., and Hoover, H.D. (1991). Quality control in the development and use of performance assessment. *Applied Measurement in Education, 4*(4), 289-303.

Duràn, R. (2001). *NAEP assessment of English language learners.* Paper prepared for Workshop on Reporting Test Results for Accommodated Test Examinees: Policy Measurement and Score Use Considerations, November 28, Washington, DC.

Education Week. (2004). Quality counts 2004: Count me in: Special education in an era of standards. *23*(17) January 8.

Elliott, S.N., Kratochwill, T.R., and McKevitt, B.C. (2001). Experimental analysis of the effects of testing accommodations on the scores of students with and without disabilities. *Journal of School Psychology, 39(1)*, 3-24.

Fuchs, L.S., Fuchs, D., Eaton, S.B., Hamlett, C., Binkley, E., and Crouch, R. (2000). Using objective data sources to enhance teacher judgments about test accommodations. *Exceptional Children, 67*(1), 67-81.

Fuchs, L.S., Fuchs, D., Eaton, S.B., Hamlett, C., and Karns, K. (2000). Supplementing teacher judgments of test accommodations with objective data sources. *School Psychology Review, 29*, 65-85.

Garcia, T., del Rio Paraent, L., Chen, L. Ferrara, S., Garavaglia, D., Johnson, E., Liang, J., Oppler, S. Searcy C., Shieh, Y., and Ye, Y. (2000). *Study of a dual language test booklet in 8th grade mathematics: Final report*. Washington, DC: American Institutes for Research.

Golden, L., and Sacks, L. (2001). *States' policies for including and accommodating English language learners in state assessments—Preliminary survey findings (2000-2001)*. Presentation at Workshop on Reporting Test Results for Accommodated Test Examinees: Policy Measurement and Score Use Considerations, November 28, Washington, DC.

Haertel, E.H. (2003). *Evidentiary argument and the comparability of scores from standard versus nonstandard test administrations*. Paper presented at the April meeting of the National Council on Measurement in Education, Chicago, IL.

Hafner, A.L. (2001). *Evaluating the impact of test accommodations on test scores of LEP students and non-LEP students*. Paper presented at the annual meeting of the American Educational Research Association, April, Seattle, WA.

Hakuta, K., Butler, Y.G., and Witt, D. (1999). *How long does it take English language learners to attain proficiency?* Unpublished manuscript, Stanford University, CA.

Hansen, E.G., and Steinberg, L.S. (2004). *Evidence centered assessment design for reasoning about testing accommodations in NAEP reading and math*. Paper commissioned by the Committee on Participation of English Language Learners and Students with Disabilities in NAEP and Other Large-Scale Assessments of the Board on Testing and Assessment of the National Academy of Sciences.

Hansen, E.G., Mislevy, R.J., and Steinberg, L.S. (2003). *Evidence-centered assessment design and individuals with disabilities*. Paper presented at the National Council on Measurement in Education Annual Meeting, April, Chicago, IL.

Hardman, M.L., Drew, C.J., and Egan, M.W. (1996). *Human exceptionality, 5th edition*. Boston, MA: Allyn and Bacon.

Hehir, T. (1996). Office of Special Education policy letter. *Individuals with Disabilities Education Report, 23*, 341.

Helwig, R., and Tindal, G. (2003). An experimental analysis of accommodation decisions on large-scale mathematics tests. *Exceptional Children, 69*, 211-225.

Huesman, R.L., and Frisbie, D. (2000). *The validity of ITBS reading comprehension test scores for learning disabled and non learning disabled students under extended-time conditions*. Paper presented at the Annual Meeting of the National Council on Measurement in Education, April, New Orleans, LA.

Johnson, E. (2000). The effects of accommodations on performance assessments. *Remedial and Special Education, 21*(5), 261-267.

Johnson, E. (2001). *Observations on the National Academies Board on Testing and Assessment Workshop on Reporting Results for Accommodated Examinees*. Paper prepared for Workshop on Reporting Test Results for Accommodated Test Examinees: Policy Measurement and Score Use Considerations, November 28, Washington, DC.

Johnson, E., Kimball, K., Brown, S.O., and Anderson, D. (2001) American sign language as an accommodation during standards-based assessments. *Assessment for Effective Intervention, 26*(2), 39-47.

Kane, M. (1992). An argument-based approach to validity. *Psychological Bulletin, 112*(3), 527-535.

Kane, M., Crooks, T., and Cohen, A. (1999). Validating measures of performance. *Educational Measurement: Issues and Practice, 18*(2), 5-17.

Kindler, A. (2002). *Survey of the states' limited English proficient students and available educational programs and services 2000-2001 summary report.* Washington, DC: National Clearinghouse for English Language Acquisition.

Koretz, D., and Hamilton, L. (2000). Assessing students with disabilities in Kentucky: Inclusion, student performance, and validity. *Educational Evaluation and Policy Analysis, 22*(3), 255-272.

Koretz, D., and Hamilton, L. (2001, April). *The performance of students with disabilities on New York's revised regents comprehensive examination in English.* (CSE Tech. Rep. No. 540). Los Angeles, CA: Center for the Study of Evaluation, Graduate School of Education and Information Studies, University of California.

Kosciolek, S., and Ysseldyke, J.E. (2000). *Effects of a reading accommodation on the validity of a reading test.* (Technical Report 28). Minneapolis: University of Minnesota, National Center on Educational Outcomes. Available: http://education.umn.edu/NCEO/OnlinePubs/Technical28.htm [January 2003].

Malouf, D. (2001). *Discussion and synthesis.* Paper prepared for Workshop on Reporting Test Results for Accommodated Test Examinees: Policy Measurement and Score Use Considerations, November 28, Washington, DC.

Mazzeo, J., Carlson, J.E., Voelkl, K.E., and Lutkus, A.D. (2000). *Increasing the participation of special needs students in NAEP: A report on 1996 NAEP research activities.* (NCES Publication No. 2000-473). Washington, DC: National Center for Education Statistics.

McKevitt, B.C., and Elliott, S.N. (in press). *The effects and consequences of using test accommodations on a standardized reading test.* Manuscript submitted for publication.

McKevitt, B.C., Marquart, A.M., Mroch, A.A., Schulte, A., Elliott, S., and Kratochwill, T. (2000). *Understanding the effects of testing accommodations: a single-case approach.* A paper presented at the annual meeting of the National Association of School Psychologists, New Orleans, LA.

Meloy, L., Deville, C., and Frisbie, D. (2000). *The effects of a reading accommodation on standardized test scores of learning disabled and non learning disabled students.* A paper presented for the National Council on Measurement in Education Annual Meeting, April, New Orleans, LA.

Messick, S. (1989). Validity. In R.L. Linn (Ed.), *Educational measurement* (3rd ed., pp. 13-103). New York: American Council on Education and Macmillan.

Messick, S. (1994). The interplay of evidence and consequences in the validation of performance assessments. *Educational Researcher, 23*(2), 13-23.

Mislevy, R.J. (1996). Test theory reconceived. *Journal of Educational Measurement, 33*(4), 379-416.

Mislevy, R.J., Steinberg, L.S., and Almond, R.G. (2002). Design and analysis in task-based language assessment. *Language Testing, 19*(4), 477-496.

Mislevy, R.J., Steinberg, L.S., and Almond, R.G. (2003). On the structure of educational assessments. *Measurement: Interdisciplinary Research and Perspectives, 1*(1), 3-62.

National Assessment Governing Board. (2001). *Mathematics framework for 2005: Pre-publication edition.* Washington, DC: Author.

National Assessment Governing Board. (2002a). *Reading framework for the 2003 national assessment of educational progress.* Washington, DC: Author.

National Assessment Governing Board. (2002b, March) *Using the National Assessment of Education Progress to confirm state test results, Report of the Ad Hoc Committee on Confirming Test Results.* Washington, DC: Author.

National Center for Education Statistics. (2003a). *NAEP questions.* Washington, DC: Author.

National Center for Education Statistics. (2003b). *Scoring guide.* Washington, DC: Author.

National Clearinghouse for English Language Acquisition and Language Instructional Programs. (2004). A national literacy panel to conduct a comprehensive evidence-based review of the research literature on the development of literacy among language minority children and youth. (A panel presentation by Diane August, Center for Applied Linguistics.) Available: http://www.ncela.gwu.edu [June 2004].

National Research Council. (1997a). *Educating one and all: students with disabilities and standards-based reform.* Committee on Goals 2000 and the Inclusion of Students with Disabilities. Lorraine M. McDonnell, Margaret J. McLaughlin, and Patricia Morison, editors. Board on Testing and Assessment, Commission on Behavioral and Social Sciences and Education. Washington, DC: National Academy Press.

National Research Council. (1997b). *Improving schooling for language-minority children: A research agenda.* Committee on Developing a Research Agenda on the Education of Limited-English-Proficient and Bilingual Students. D. August and K. Hakuta, editors. Board on Children, Youth, and Families, Commission on Behavioral and Social Sciences and Education. Washington, DC: National Academy Press.

National Research Council. (1999a). *Grading the nation's report card: Research from the evaluation of NAEP.* Committee on the Evaluation of National and State Assessments of Educational Progress. Nambury S. Raju, James W. Pellegrino, Meryl W. Bertenthal, Karen J. Mitchell, and Lee R. Jones, editors. Board on Testing and Assessment, Commission on Behavioral and Social Sciences and Education. Washington, DC: National Academy Press.

National Research Council. (1999b). *Uncommon measures: Equivalence and linkage among educational tests.* Committee on Equivalency and Linkage of Educational Tests. Committee on Equivalency and Linkage of Educational Tests. Michael J. Feuer, Paul W. Holland, Bert F. Green, Meryl W. Bertenthal, and F. Cadelle Hemphill, editors. Board on Testing and Assessment, Commission on Behavioral and Social Sciences and Education. Washington, DC: National Academy Press.

National Research Council. (2000a). *Reporting district-level NAEP data: Summary of a workshop.* Committee on NAEP Reporting Practices. Pasquale DeVito and Judith A. Koenig, editors. Board on Testing and Assessment, Commission on Behavioral and Social Sciences and Education. Washington, DC: National Academy Press.

National Research Council. (2000b). *Testing English-language learners in U.S. schools: Report and workshop summary.* Committee on Educational Excellence and Testing Equity, Kenji Hakuta and Alexandra Beatty, editors. Center for Education. Washington, DC: National Academy Press.

National Research Council. (2002a). *Minority students in special and gifted education.* Committee on Minority Representation in Special Education, M. Suzanne Donovan and Christopher T. Cross, editors. Division of Behavioral and Social Sciences and Education. Washington, DC: The National Academies Press.

National Research Council. (2002b). *Reporting test results for students with disabilities and English-language learners: Summary of a workshop.* Judith Anderson Koenig, editor. Board on Testing and Assessment, Center for Education, Division of Behavioral and Social Sciences and Education. Washington, DC: The National Academies Press.

Rivera, C., and Stansfield, C.W. (2001). *The effects of linguistic simplification of science test items on performance of limited English proficient and monolingual English-speaking students.* Paper presented at the annual meeting of the American Educational Research Association, April, Seattle, WA.

Rivera, C., Stansfield, C.W., Scialdone, L., and Sharkey, M. (2000). *An analysis of state policies for the inclusion and accommodation of English language learners in state assessment programs during 1998-1999.* Arlington, VA: George Washington University Center for Equity and Excellence in Education.

Runyan, M.K. (1991). The effect of extra time on reading comprehension scores for university students with and without learning disabilities. *Journal of Learning Disabilities, 24*, 104-108.

Schulte, A.A., Elliott, S.N., and Kratochwill, T.R. (2001). *Effects of testing accommodations on standardized mathematics test scores: An experimental analysis of the performances of students with and without disabilities.* Unpublished manuscript, University of Wisconsin-Madison.

Shavelson, R.J., Baxter, G.P., and Gao, X. (1993). Sampling variability of performance assessments. *Journal of Educational Measurement, 30*, 215-232.

Shepard, L., Taylor, G., and Betebenner, D. (1998). *Inclusion of limited-English-proficient students in Rhode Island's grade 4 mathematics performance assessment.* Los Angeles: University of California, Center for the Study of Evaluation/National Center for Research on Evaluation, Standards, and Student Testing.

Sireci, S., Li, S., and Scarpati, S. (2003). *The effects of test accommodation on test performance: A review of the literature.* (Center for Educational Assessment Research Report no. 485). Amherst, MA: School of Education, University of Massachusetts.

Solano-Flores, G., and Trumbull, E. (2003). Examining language in context: The need for new research and practice paradigms in the testing of English-language learners. *Educational Researcher, 32*(2), 3-13.

Taylor, C. (1997). *The effect of school expenditure on the achievement of high school students: Evidence from NELS and the CCD.* Paper presented at the American Education Research Association annual meeting, April, Chicago.

Taylor, W. (2002). *Analysis of provisions of ESEA relating to assessment.* Paper prepared for March 22 meeting of the Board on Testing and Assessment, Washington, DC.

Thompson, S., Blount, A., and Thurlow, M. (2002). *A summary of research on the effects of test accommodations: 1999 through 2001* (Technical Report 34). Minneapolis: University of Minnesota, National Center on Educational Outcomes. Available: http://education.umn.edu/NCEO/OnlinePubs/Technical34.htm [January 2003].

Thurlow, M.L., Elliott, J.L., and Ysseldyke, J.E. (2002). *Testing students with disabilities: Practical strategies for complying with district and state requirements.* Thousand Oaks, CA: Corwin Press.

Thurlow, M.L., Wiley, H.I., and Bielinski, J. (2002). *Biennial performance reports: 2000-2001 state assessment data.* Minneapolis: University of Minnesota, National Center on Educational Outcomes.

Tindal, G., and Fuchs, L. (2000) *A summary of research on test changes: An empirical basis for defining accommodations.* Lexington: University of Kentucky, Mid-South Regional Resource Center Interdisciplinary Human Development Institute.

Tindal, G., Anderson, L., Helwig, R., Miller, S., and Glasgow, A. (1998). Accommodating students with learning disabilities on math tests using language simplification. *Exceptional Children, 64*(4), 439-450.

Tindal, G., Heath, B., Hollenbeck, K., Almond, P., and Harniss, M. (1998). Accommodating students with disabilities on large-scale tests: An experimental study, *Exceptional Children, 64(4)*, 439-450.

Toulmin, S.E. (1958). *The uses of argument.* Cambridge, England: Cambridge University Press.

U.S. Department of Education. (2002). *24th annual report to Congress on the implementation of the Individuals with Disabilities Education Act.* Washington, DC: Author.

U.S. Department of Education National Center for Education Statistics. (1997). *The inclusion of students with disabilities and limited English proficient students in large-scale assessments: A summary of recent progress.* (NCES 97-482). Washington, DC: Author.

U.S. Department of Education National Center for Education Statistics and Office of Educational Research and Improvement. (2001). *The NAEP 1998 technical report.* (NCES 2001-509). Washington, DC: Author.

U.S. Department of Education National Center for Education Statistics and Office of Educational Research and Improvement. (2003). *NAEP 2003 assessment administrator manual.* Washington, DC: Author.

U.S. Department of Education National Center for Education Statistics and Institute of Education Sciences. (2003). *The nation's report card: Reading 2002.* (NCES 2003-521). Washington, DC: Author.

Walz, L., Albus, D., Thompson, S., and Thurlow, M. (2000). *Effect of a multiple day test accommodation on the performance of special education students.* (NCEO Report 34). Minneapolis: University of Minnesota, National Center on Educational Outcomes.

Weston, T.J. (2002). *The validity of oral accommodation in testing.* (NCES 200306). Washington, DC: National Center for Education Statistics.

Wightman, L.F. (1993). *Test takers with disabilities: A summary of data from special administrations of the LSAT.* (LSAC Research Report 93-03). Newtown, PA: Law School Admission Council.

Willingham, W.W., Ragosta, M., Bennett, R.E., Braun, H., Rock, D.A., and Powers, D.E. (1988). *Testing handicapped people.* Boston, MA: Allyn and Bacon.

Zehr, M.A. (2004). Paige softens rules on English-language learners. *Education Week, 23*(24), 25.

Zettel, J. (1982). Implementing the right to a free appropriate public education. In *Special education in America: Its legal and governmental foundations,* J. Ballard, B. Ramirez and F. Weintraub, editors. Reston, VA: Council for Exceptional Children.

Ziomek, R.L., and Andrews, K.M. (1996). *Predicting the college grade point averages of special-tested students from their ACT assessment scores and high school grades.* (ACT Research Report 96-7). Iowa City, IA: ACT.

Ziomek, R.L., and Andrews, K.M. (1998). *ACT Assessment score gains of special-tested students who tested at least twice.* (Report No. ACT-RR-98-8). Iowa City, IA: ACT.

Zurcher, R., and Bryant, D.P. (2001). The validity and comparability of entrance examination scores after accommodations are made for students with LD. *Journal of Learning Disabilities, 34*(5), 462-471.

Zuriff, G.E. (2000). Extra examination time for students with learning disabilities: An examination of the maximum potential thesis. *Applied Measurement in Education, 13*(1), 99-117.

Zwick, R. (2002). *Fair game? The use of standardized admissions tests in higher education.* New York: RoutledgeFalmer.

Appendix

Biographical Sketches of Committee Members and Staff

Lyle F. Bachman is professor and chair, Department of Applied Linguistics and TESL, University of California, Los Angeles. He is a past president of the American Association for Applied Linguistics and of the International Language Testing Association and is currently coeditor, with Charles Alderson, of the *Cambridge Language Assessment Series*. He was the first winner of the TESOL/ Newbury House Award for Outstanding Research, has won the Modern Language Association of Americaís Kenneth Mildenberger Award for outstanding research publication twice, and has been given the Lifetime Achievement Award by the International Language Testing Association. He has published numerous articles and books in the areas of language testing, program evaluation, and second language acquisition. He regularly conducts research projects in language testing and program design and evaluation, as well as practitioner training workshops in language assessment, both at American institutions and at institutions abroad. His current research interests include validation theory, linking current validation models and procedures to test use, issues in assessing the academic achievement and academic English of ELs in schools, the interface between language testing research and second language acquisition research, and the dialectic of constructs and contexts in language testing and educational performance assessment.

Alexandra S. Beatty is a senior program officer at the Center for Education. She has served as the staff director for the Committee on Educational Excellence and Testing Equity, which has issued reports on the testing of English language learners and on measuring dropout rates, and has been a member of the staff of the Board on Testing and Assessment and also the Board on International Comparative Studies in Education. Prior to joining the NRC, she coordinated the National Assessment of Educational Progress (NAEP) in U.S. history for the Educational Testing Service (ETS) in Princeton, NJ, and worked on a number of other NAEP programs and other testing programs at ETS. Ms. Beatty received a B.A. in philosophy from Williams College and an M.A. in history from Bryn Mawr College.

Jonathan G. Dings serves as chief of Planning and Assessment for the Boulder Valley School District, where he started working in 1998 as the director of Assessment. His major duties include directing district administration and reporting results of the Colorado Student Assessment Program and other standardized tests, as well as surveys of student and staff attitude and parent satisfaction. In the four years prior to working for Boulder Valley, he worked for the Kentucky Department of Education, most recently as group leader, psychometric analysis with responsibility for evaluating the psychometric characteristics of the Kentucky Instructional Results Information System. Dr. Dings earned his Ph.D. in educational measurement and statistics from the University of Iowa in 1997 and has served on several state technical advisory committees.

Judy L. Elliott is currently the assistant superintendent of Special Education in the Long Beach Unified School District, Long Beach, California, the third largest urban school system in the state with approximately 97,000 students. Formerly a senior researcher at the National Center on Educational Outcomes, she worked and continues to assist districts and state departments of education in their efforts to update and realign curriculum frameworks, instruction, and assessments to include all students. Her research interests focus on effective instruction, IEP development and its alignment with standards and assessments, decision making for accountability, accommodation, and assessment as well as translating information on standards and assessments for various audiences including parents, teachers, school boards, and other community groups. Dr. Elliott continues to serve as a national consultant and staff development professional for school districts and organizations. She has trained staff, teachers, and administrators, both in the South Pacific and the United States, in areas including linking assessment to instruction and intervention; strategies and tactics for effective instruction; curriculum modification for students with disabilities; intervention and teacher assistance teams; authentic and curriculum-based evaluation; instructional environment evaluation; collaborative teaching; strategies for difficult-to-manage students; and accountability and assessment practices.

Judith Anderson Koenig is a senior program officer with the NRC's Board on Testing and Assessment and has worked on a number of projects related to NAEP as well as projects on teacher licensing and adult literacy. She began her career as a special education teacher and diagnostician, working primarily with learning disabled students. Prior to joining the NRC, she was a senior research associate with the Association of American Medical Colleges where she worked on students with the Medical College Admission Test. She received a Ph.D. in educational measurement, statistics, and evaluation from the University of Maryland.

Margaret J. McLaughlin is a professor in the Department of Special Education and associate director of the Institute for the Study of Exceptional Children and Youth. She is currently involved in several projects, one of which is the Educational Policy Research Reform Institute, a research institute focused on accountability and students with disabilities. Dr. McLaughlin has conducted research related to standards-driven reform and students with disabilities for over 15 years. She served on the Board on Testing and Assessment (BOTA) Committee on Minority Representation in Special Education, the Committee on Reporting Results for Accommodated Test Takers: Policy and Technical Considerations, and the Technical Panel on Special Education Finance. She was cochair of the BOTA Committee on Goals 2000 and the Inclusion of Students with Disabilities. She has written extensively on issues related to the interaction between special education policies and state and federal educational reforms. Dr. McLaughlin began her career as a teacher of emotionally disturbed/autistic children and students with learning disabilities. Dr. McLaughlin received a Ph.D. in special education from the University of Virginia.

Mark D. Reckase is a professor of measurement and quantitative methods in the Department of Counseling, Educational Psychology and Special Education at Michigan State University. His research focuses on modeling of the interaction of persons and test items; multidimensional models of the persons item interaction; and computer applications to measurement of cognitive skills. He has numerous publications on requirements, values, validity, appropriateness, reliability, computerization, and modeling of assessment. He received a Ph.D. in psychology from Syracuse University.

Lourdes C. Rovira is the assistant superintendent for Curriculum and Instruction in Miami-Dade County Public Schools (M-DCPS), the fourth largest school district in the United States. In this capacity, Dr. Rovira oversees a multitude of programs and initiatives aimed at ensuring that students graduating from M-DCPS have the necessary skills to enter the workforce of the twenty-first century. In addition to serving on various educational advisory councils, Dr. Rovira has served as consultant to other school districts, institutions of higher education, the Council of Great City Schools, and publishing companies. As a champion for the rights of immigrant students and second language learners, Dr. Rovira's expertise is sought by educators and journalists from all over the world.

María Medina Seidner, former director of Bilingual Education at the Texas Education Agency, has worked in bilingual education for 30 years. She was director of bilingual education for the state of Illinois for 15 years after having worked as director of the Bilingual Education Service Center for Illinois and the Midwest. María has also taught French and Spanish in high school and college. A native of Puerto Rico, she came to Texas as a high school student and earned B.A. and M.A. degrees from the University of Texas in Austin. During her career, she has been active in various professional organizations and has served as president of the National Advisory Council on Bilingual Education. Her current responsibilities are varied and complex but they all have the goal of insuring that schools in Texas provide appropriate and successful educational programs for students of limited English proficiency.

Rebecca Zwick is a professor of education at the University of California, Santa Barbara. She specializes in applied statistics and educational testing. Previously, she spent 12 years in the Statistical and Psychometric Research Division at Educational Testing Service (ETS) in Princeton, New Jersey. She serves on several national advisory panels and on the Board of Directors of the National Council on Measurement in Education, and is vice president for the Measurement and Research Methodology Division of the American Educational Research Association. Dr. Zwick worked on National Assessment of Education Progress (NAEP) data analyses for seven years while at ETS. She served on the BOTA Committee on Embedding Common Test Items in State and District Assessments and currently serves on the NAEP design and analysis committee. Dr. Zwick received a Ph.D. in education from the University of California, Berkeley.